180 Bible Verses for

CONQUERING
ANXIETY

180 Bible Verses for

CONQUERING ANXIETY

Devotions for Women

CAREY SCOTT

BARBOUR
PUBLISHING

Print ISBN 978-1-64352-961-5

Published by Barbour Publishing, Inc., 1810 Barbour Drive, Uhrichsville, Ohio 44683, www.barbourbooks.com

Our mission is to inspire the world with the life-changing message of the Bible.

Member of the
Evangelical Christian
Publishers Association

Printed in the United States of America.

Introduction

Anxiety is something we will all face in our lifetime. You might battle it every now and again, or maybe it's a constant companion that never leaves you alone. Either way, the hope for the freedom you desire can be found in the powerful Word of God. In its pages, you will discover the much-needed peace that often eludes you. You will be encouraged to trust the Lord rather than entertain fear and worry. And your faith will grow as His truths sink deep into your heart. Let this book be a daily guide that reminds you to trust God more than the circumstances causing anxiety. And watch how time spent in scripture gives you strength to stand strong.

Where Is Your Focus?

*"Let me give you a new command: Love
one another. In the same way I loved you,
you love one another. This is how everyone
will recognize that you are my disciples—
when they see the love you have for each other."*
JOHN 13:34–35 MSG

We feel anxious because we are focused on ourselves. We are locked in on the things that frustrate and discourage us. In our tunnel vision, we see only what's intimidating and overwhelming. And we end up spiraling into a pit of despair. Who wouldn't freak out if they sat in their own worry? It's debilitating! But what if we lifted our heads and looked at the needs of the world around us instead? What if we stopped fixating on ourselves and found ways to bless others? Ask God to reveal ways to help those around you. It will take your mind off yourself and point others to Him.

Feelings Don't Negate Facts

*For God will never give you the spirit
of fear, but the Holy Spirit who gives
you mighty power, love, and self-control.*
2 TIMOTHY 1:7 TPT

We weren't created to live with fear, but that rarely stops us from being racked with worry and anxiety. From relationships to finances to health, fear creeps in and robs us of peace. And the idea that we can access power, love, and self-control often feels inadequate. In our weakness, it feels unattainable. But friend, those feelings don't negate the truth. They may be real feelings, but that doesn't mean they're facts. Did you know God addresses anxiety more than 350 times in the Bible because He knew it would be a struggle? In those anxious moments, cry out for His help. Share your stress, and ask for His peace. He is always there.

Pour Out Your Heart

Trust in, lean on, rely on, and have confidence in Him at all times, you people; pour out your hearts before Him. God is a refuge for us (a fortress and a high tower).

PSALM 62:8 AMPC

When we're worried and weary, there is no safer place for us to go than to the Lord. He is the only One who sees the depth of our fear and knows exactly what we need. He understands the complexity of our stress. God is trustworthy, and He invites us into His comfort. He provides a safe place for us to be vulnerable with how we're feeling. And unlike the world, God's love is perfect and steadfast, without criticism or exasperation. That means we can place our deepest, darkest anxieties on Him. We can share the truth of what scares us. And we can be honest about the insecurities we're facing.

#4

Don't Speak

*"God will fight the battle for you.
And you? You keep your mouths shut!"*
EXODUS 14:14 MSG

Have you ever noticed that when we get stressed out, we talk a lot? We ruminate with our friends about the cause of our anxiety. We complain to our family, trying to garner compassion. We post about it on social media, looking for sympathy. We spend an awful lot of time unpacking the pressure we're feeling. And while your voice matters and it's healthy to talk things through with those you trust, maybe God is asking you to pull back a bit. Maybe He is asking you to trust Him. Ask the Lord to tell you your role in the battle. Is this one where you're taking the next step forward as He leads? Or is this a time when you are silent, watching the Father work it out Himself?

#5

Not Your Own Savior

People cannot save themselves.
But with God, all things are possible.
MATTHEW 19:26 VOICE

It's stressful when we decide to figure things out on our own. Without even realizing it, we often put all the pressure on ourselves to find the answers. We think it's up to us to come up with a solution. Rather than ask for help, we try to fix our problems solo. And when we can't, we feel like failures and beat ourselves up. Our hearts are full of anxiety as we worry about the details. But God knows we have limitations because He created us. He never planned for us to be our own saviors. Instead, the Lord planned to work with us to make things possible. It's a partnership. Next time, remember to take the pressure off yourself by asking God to help.

#6

Undone

"Are you tired? Worn out? Burned out on religion? Come to me. Get away with me and you'll recover your life. I'll show you how to take a real rest. Walk with me and work with me—watch how I do it. Learn the unforced rhythms of grace. I won't lay anything heavy or ill-fitting on you. Keep company with me and you'll learn to live freely and lightly."
MATTHEW 11:28–30 MSG

Life is hard and exhausting. We pack our day trying to be everything to everyone. In the end, we feel as though we are under water as we try to over-achieve. And when one thing goes wrong, we lose it. We're undone. Our stress level is off the charts, and we're miserable. Did you know that God is ready to take that anxiety off your shoulders right now? He is offering to take your worries and exchange them for rest. Why not talk to Him about it? He's listening.

A Wrap-Around Presence

I am standing in absolute stillness, silent before the one I love, waiting as long as it takes for him to rescue me. Only God is my Savior, and he will not fail me. For he alone is my safe place. His wrap-around presence always protects me as my champion defender. There's no risk of failure with God! So why would I let worry paralyze me, even when troubles multiply around me?

PSALM 62:5–6 TPT

Take a moment to visualize God's presence wrapping around you in a stressful situation. When you're facing fear, imagine Him engulfing you like a weighted blanket. Think about how the anxiety would melt away and you would feel safe and secure. Let this image be close in those times when you feel vulnerable. Let this truth be what calms you when worry begins to creep in. In those moments when you're uneasy or concerned, ask the Lord to wrap around you and deliver peace.

God Is Nearer

*God is our shelter and our strength. When troubles
seem near, God is nearer, and He's ready to help.
So why run and hide? No fear, no pacing, no biting
fingernails. When the earth spins out of control,
we are sure and fearless. When mountains crumble
and the waters run wild, we are sure and fearless.*
PSALM 46:1–2 VOICE

No matter what troubles are knocking at your door,
regardless of the challenges you're facing right
now, even when everything feels hopeless and
you're stressed to the max, although you're terrified at how it will all work out, have faith that God
is near. He is closer than any problem or concern.
He is closer to you than the anxiety that's eating
you up. And the Lord promises to help. Let Him be
your shelter and your strength when mountains
crumble and waters run wild. He will calm you and
bring peace every time.

The Stress of Obsession

*Don't be obsessed with getting more material
things. Be relaxed with what you have.
Since God assured us, "I'll never let you down,
never walk off and leave you," we can boldly
quote, God is there, ready to help; I'm fearless
no matter what. Who or what can get to me?*
HEBREWS 13:5–6 MSG

Do you ever feel like you're just trying to keep up
with those around you? Every time your friends
upgrade their things, you feel a tug to do the same.
Most of the time, that feeling is a reflex. We're con-
ditioned to be obsessed with what others have,
thanks to the world we live in. It's a longing baked
into us at a young age and that continues into adult-
hood. But God is asking us to be content with what
we have, letting His presence be what we long for
above all else. He knows that contentment will satisfy and embolden.

#10

Every Morning

*It is because of the Lord's mercy and
loving-kindness that we are not consumed,
because His [tender] compassions fail not.
They are new every morning; great and
abundant is Your stability and faithfulness.*
LAMENTATIONS 3:22–23 AMPC

Each night as you lay your head on the pillow, tell
the Lord all the stressors the day brought your way.
Don't leave anything out. Be honest and share your
heart. Tell Him what scares you. Tell Him what
insecurities popped up that day. Tell Him what
caused you anxiety and concern. Use this time to
purge yourself of everything that brought on worry.
Trust that He not only wants to hear every detail
but is already working things out on your behalf.
Even more, remember that God is compassionate
and caring, and every morning He's ready to help
you navigate another day of stress. Let Him be your
faithful companion and stabilizing force.

The Power of His Love

Then you will be empowered to discover what every holy one experiences—the great magnitude of the astonishing love of Christ in all its dimensions. How deeply intimate and far-reaching is his love! How enduring and inclusive it is! Endless love beyond measurement that transcends our understanding—this extravagant love pours into you until you are filled to overflowing with the fullness of God!

EPHESIANS 3:18–19 TPT

If you really knew how much the Lord loved you, it would transform your response to stress. It would empower you to trust He is in the details of your situation. You'd be calmed, knowing God has a complete understanding of what's causing your anxiety. Understanding His unending and inexhaustible love would enable you to hold on to peace even in the most destabilizing moments. But because of our human limitations, it's almost impossible to grasp. This is where faith comes in. Choose to believe what the Bible says about God's love, and ask Him to reinforce this truth in your life.

#12

With You Till the End

*Then disciple them. Form them in the
practices and postures that I have taught you,
and show them how to follow the commands
I have laid down for you. And I will be with you,
day after day, to the end of the age.*
MATTHEW 28:20 VOICE

Just as Jesus promised the disciples to be with them
until the end, He makes the same promise to you.
No matter what happens, you can believe the Lord
won't leave you. You never have to figure out life on
your own. God will always be there, no matter what.
Do you know what that does for an anxious heart?
It brings instant peace. Think about it. If the One
who created heaven and earth and everything in
between is fully committed to walking through life
with you, you can exhale. So, breathe in His faithfulness and release the stress.

Nothing Stands in His Way

*You're kind and tenderhearted to those who
don't deserve it and very patient with people
who fail you. Your love is like a flooding river
overflowing its banks with kindness.*
PSALM 145:8 TPT

Sometimes it's hard to pray because we feel guilty
about what we said to another in the heat of the
moment. We're ashamed by our actions, and we
worry that we've pushed God too far and He's
done with us. We end up super stressed, feeling
hopeless about what comes next. But in those moments, remember that the Lord doesn't think the
way we think. He doesn't hold resentment like we
do. And when we need Him, nothing stands in His
way. God's love drives His response to you. His love
is full and complete, unchanging, and unshakable.
Don't let any stress or worry keep you from reach-
ing out to Him.

#14

You're Forgiven

But if we own up to our sins, God shows that He is faithful and just by forgiving us of our sins and purifying us from the pollution of all the bad things we have done.

1 JOHN 1:9 VOICE

You don't have to stress about all the bad things you have done. They don't have any power over you anymore. Maybe you're worried because you have decided your past is uglier than most and God's forgiveness doesn't reach that far, but that simply isn't true. You're not the one person He can't extend grace to; it doesn't work that way. Instead, the Lord is inviting you into peace by asking you to own up to your sins. He knows confession is a mighty de-stressor. And even more, He promises complete forgiveness. You'll be purified from the anxiety of carrying around the weight of bad decisions and choices.

Saturated

Don't be pulled in different directions or worried about a thing. Be saturated in prayer throughout each day, offering your faith-filled requests before God with overflowing gratitude. Tell him every detail of your life, then God's wonderful peace that transcends human understanding, will make the answers known to you through Jesus Christ.
PHILIPPIANS 4:6–7 TPT

Prayer unlocks peace every time. In those moments when you feel pulled in a million directions and overwhelmed by it all, talk to God. When you're scared about the next step or worried about the *what-ifs* ahead, share your concerns with the Lord. Every time your heart starts racing from bad news, unpack it with God. Stress may be your first response, but it doesn't have to hold you prisoner. As a matter of fact, the Lord is always available to hear every detail of what's causing stress. Tell Him what scares you, the insecurities you're facing, and the pressure that's mounting, and then feel the peace begin to saturate your troubled heart.

#16

The Stress of Discontentment

*So be content with who you are, and don't put on
airs. God's strong hand is on you; he'll promote
you at the right time. Live carefree before
God; he is most careful with you.*
1 Peter 5:6–7 msg

When you aren't happy with yourself, it's stressful.
Think about it. When you feel lousy about the way
you look, you're worried what others may think.
When you missed a deadline at work, you're worried about your job security. When you scream at
the kids in a bad parenting moment, you're stressed
it may cause irreparable damage. And in the end,
you feel like a failure or a fraud. Deep breath,
friend. God never requests or expects flawless
living. He knows you're going to mess up, and He
wants you to know you're loved no matter what. A
bad day doesn't make a bad person, and when you
take that stress to Him, He'll remind you of that.

Don't Worry

"Therefore, I say to you, don't worry about your life, what you'll eat or what you'll drink, or about your body, what you'll wear. Isn't life more than food and the body more than clothes? . . . Who among you by worrying can add a single moment to your life?"
MATTHEW 6:25, 27 CEB

It's easy to stress about life's details. We worry about what we'll make for dinner, hoping everyone will like it. We worry about finding the perfect clothes for picture day at the kids' school. We worry about the medical bills that keep piling up. We worry about the effects of aging and how it makes us look. What do you worry about? Your faith activated is what will stop this kind of stress. When you choose to believe that God will keep His promises and take care of you, it deflates the anxiety that rages inside. His constant message is to trust Him. He knows your needs, and He will meet every one of them.

Perfect Peace

*"Peace I leave with you; My [perfect] peace
I give to you; not as the world gives do I give
to you. Do not let your heart be troubled,
nor let it be afraid. [Let My perfect peace
calm you in every circumstance and give you
courage and strength for every challenge.]"*

JOHN 14:27 AMP

What brings you peace? How do you settle your
nerves? For some, they stay busy and avoid dealing
with the issues. Some feed their stress with food or
alcohol. Others employ retail therapy to feel better.
Yet others let books or movies take them to another
world. The problem is that these escapes don't last
for long. They are substitutes for the perfect peace
that comes from God. The world has offerings, but
none matches His antidote for an anxious heart.
Every time you feel the stress of life, be quick to talk
to God about it. Ask Him for what you need.

#19

You're Not Made to Be a Stress-Case

You see, God did not give us a cowardly spirit but a powerful, loving, and disciplined spirit.

2 TIMOTHY 1:7 VOICE

In those moments when you feel gutless and spineless because of fear, stress, and insecurity, remind yourself this feeling isn't from God. Say it out loud. Declare it. Why? Because sometimes the best way to learn is audibly. We have to hear it to believe it. And when we begin to believe, it strengthens our resolve. That determination gives us courage, and courage gives us confidence to believe we are who God says we are. He didn't create us to be a stress-case. He never wanted us to cower from anxiety. Instead, the Lord equipped us with a powerful spirit that is disciplined to trust the One who made us. There may be many opportunities to worry every day, but you have a choice in how you respond. Choose wisely.

It's a Command, Not a Suggestion

"Have I not commanded you? Be strong and courageous! Do not be terrified or dismayed (intimidated), for the LORD your God is with you wherever you go."

JOSHUA 1:9 AMP

Did you catch that God commanded rather than suggested? He didn't recommend courage and bravery. It wasn't hinted at or insinuated. God didn't imply it. No, it was—it is—nonnegotiable. His words are laced with authority and power. It's also important to realize this command isn't to be fulfilled on our own. It's the Lord's presence that will bolster us. We don't have to let the stress of the situation overtake us, because we can be confident knowing we're not alone. God promises to walk through those anxiety-ridden circumstances with us, supernaturally increasing our strength and courage when we need it. There is no reason to be worried, terrified, or dismayed, because you have God on your side.

The Promise to Restore

*And then, after your brief suffering, the God of
all loving grace, who has called you to share in his
eternal glory in Christ, will personally and powerfully
restore you and make you stronger than ever. Yes,
he will set you firmly in place and build you up.*

1 PETER 5:10 TPT

It's a relief to know that God promises to restore us
after a season of suffering. He will use the stresses
and struggles we face to grow us into women of
strength. The Lord never wastes a moment, and
He is committed to turning the ashes of your life
into something beautiful. All the anxiety you may
be feeling will not only be short-lived, but it will
be used for your benefit and God's glory. He will
make everything right as He keeps you from falling,
secures you in place, and builds you up. You can
fully rely on and trust in Him.

Piling It on God

*Pile your troubles on G*OD*'s shoulders—he'll carry your load, he'll help you out. He'll never let good people topple into ruin. But you, God, will throw the others into a muddy bog, cut the lifespan of assassins and traitors in half. And I trust in you.*
PSALM 55:22–23 MSG

Can you see a visual of piling your troubles on God's shoulders? In your mind's eye, collect every stressor and worry, and place it on Him. Are you stressed in parenting? Is there worry at work? Is the state of your marriage a concern? Maybe your finances are troublesome? Are you navigating some difficult friendships? Are you feeling insecure or afraid? Whatever it is that's weighing you down right now, have the courage to take it off yourself and transfer it to the God who loves you. He promises to carry the load so you can find rest and peace. What a powerful and beautiful picture of surrender and sovereignty.

#23

Listen for His Voice

Trust God from the bottom of your heart;
don't try to figure out everything on your own.
Listen for God's voice in everything you do,
everywhere you go; he's the one who will keep
you on track. Don't assume that you know it all.
PROVERBS 3:5–6 MSG

Have you ever thrown your hands in the air, frustrated because the mess of your life just doesn't make sense? You think *Why me?* It feels like defeat. Failure. And no matter how hard you try, the stressful situations feel impossible to figure out. This is something we all face from time to time. We can all relate. It's a common response to the difficult situations we deal with. But God wants you to listen for His voice instead. Every day, He invites you to surrender any anxious thoughts to Him as He directs your next steps. God will always keep you on track.

God Knows

"For I know the plans I have for you,"
says the Eternal, "plans for peace, not evil,
to give you a future and hope—never forget that."
JEREMIAH 29:11 VOICE

God knows. Let those two words offer so much comfort to your weary heart. God doesn't miss a thing when it comes to you. He knows everything that's weighing you down, causing sleepless nights and worrisome days. He sees the situations that pile on the stress no matter what you do. He understands the complex feelings of worthlessness you battle every day. God is fully aware of the worry that comes from your relationships, and He sees all you've done to try and alleviate it. You're fully known and seen and loved by Him! In those tough seasons, hold on to the promise that the Lord has plans for your life—good plans full of hope. God wants goodness for you, not a pile of problems. And if you ask, He won't let stress derail your future.

Leave Tomorrow Alone

"Give your entire attention to what God is doing right now, and don't get worked up about what may or may not happen tomorrow. God will help you deal with whatever hard things come up when the time comes."
MATTHEW 6:34 MSG

This challenge to leave tomorrow's worries alone isn't easy. We are forward-thinking women who can't help but plan and organize. We have to work through schedules for our families, upcoming events, workday flow, home management, and the like. And with this comes stress because we desperately want details to fall into place. So, we obsess about what's next, and it leaves us anxious. We're taxed by the horrible outcome and ending possibilities and fixate on them. But God says to leave tomorrow alone. He wants you to stay present in today so you don't get stirred up with worry. And even more, the Lord promises to help you handle every stress in the moment. He's got you, friend.

Surrendered or Stubborn?

*I hear the Lord saying, "I will stay close to you,
instructing and guiding you along the pathway for
your life. I will advise you along the way and lead
you forth with my eyes as your guide. So don't make
it difficult; don't be stubborn when I take you where
you've not been before. Don't make me tug you
and pull you along. Just come with me!"*

Psalm 32:8–9 TPT

We get to choose whether we're part of the problem
or part of the solution. When we feel overwhelmed,
we can either trust God and follow Him or be stubborn in our own ways. In His wisdom, the Lord
is offering help. He knows the path to peace. God
promises to stay close so we hear His voice instructing and guiding us out of the chaos. He will clear
obstacles that are keeping you stirred up. And you
can either surrender to His leading or be stubborn
as you try to figure things out on your own. What
will you do?

#27

Open Up

So my conclusion is this: Many are the sorrows and frustrations of those who don't come clean with God. But when you trust in the Lord for forgiveness, his wrap-around love will surround you.

PSALM 32:10 TPT

One of the things that stresses us out the most is carrying around memories of all the wrong choices and bad decisions we've made. We worry about being judged by God and others. We worry about our reputation, certain it's been ruined by what we said or did. And we end up anxious and depressed. There is a sweet solution, you know. One that will help the sorrow and frustrations melt away so we can have peace restored. Why not open up to God about the things causing guilt and shame? Pour out your heart, and His wrap-around love will surround you. There's something so powerful about coming clean with God.

How to Calm the Panic

"Don't panic. I'm with you. There's no need to fear
for I'm your God. I'll give you strength. I'll help you.
I'll hold you steady, keep a firm grip on you."
ISAIAH 41:10 MSG

A theme we often find in the Word is how God's presence helps calm an anxious or fearful heart. Something powerful happens when we realize God is with us. Just knowing He is near brings a sense of peace and removes the lonely feelings. The next time you're feeling overwhelmed and under water, remember that God sees you. You can ask Him right then and there to help. You can ask Him to bring perspective to your panic, and you can ask the Lord to steady your emotions so you can think straight. It takes intentionality to cry out to God for help, because it's usually not our default button. But when we activate our faith and take our stress to God, He will intervene in amazing ways.

The Power of Words

*Anxiety in a man's heart weighs it down,
but a good (encouraging) word makes it glad.*
PROVERBS 12:25 AMP

We all need encouragement. Period. But we need it all the more when we're struggling with anxiety. There is so much power in just being reminded by someone that everything will be okay. It bolsters us when someone reminds us that we are not alone and that they are with us. When we hear the words *I know you can do this,* it gives us strength. There's no doubt words can carry an extraordinary blessing to a heart weighed down by stress and worry. And as much as we need that encouragement from time to time, we should quickly give it to others on the same journey. Look for those who are struggling, and speak life into their weary souls. Encourage them to stay strong, and remind them God loves them. We're in this together, right?

The Love of God

Who stood up for me against the wicked? Who took my side against evil workers? If God hadn't been there for me, I never would have made it. The minute I said, "I'm slipping, I'm falling," your love, God, took hold and held me fast. When I was upset and beside myself, you calmed me down and cheered me up.

PSALM 94:16–19 MSG

God's love is arguably the strongest force in heaven and earth. It's why He never holds a sin against you. It's why He's always there to save you and restore your broken heart. Love is why God is available to you anytime any day, and it's why you'll spend eternity with Him in heaven. But His love for you is also the greatest calming force when you're feeling troubled. Talk to Him about your heartache.

#31

We Need Wisdom

If you don't know what you're doing, pray to
the Father. He loves to help. You'll get his help,
and won't be condescended to when you ask for it.
Ask boldly, believingly, without a second thought.
People who "worry their prayers" are like wind-
whipped waves. Don't think you're going to get
anything from the Master that way, adrift at sea,
keeping all your options open.

JAMES 1:5–8 MSG

Sometimes our source of stress is that we don't know what to do next. We can't seem to figure out the best next step. So, we sit in the stress, afraid of moving forward. That's why it's so important to ask the Lord for wisdom. He understands what's going on; He knows exactly what needs to happen next to bring resolution and peace. Worrying won't do anything but stress us out and delay the solution. Accept His offer for wisdom so you can live with confidence.

Your Defense to Stress

God, have mercy on me because I'm being trampled.
All day long the enemy oppresses me. My attackers
trample me all day long because I have so many ene-
mies. Exalted one, whenever I'm afraid, I put my trust
in you—in God, whose word I praise. I trust in God;
I won't be afraid. What can mere flesh do to me?
PSALM 56:1–4 CEB

It's horrible when we feel attacked by others. Their harsh words of judgment make us doubt ourselves, and their mean-spiritedness leaves us feeling lousy. That kind of destabilizing environment creates stress, and even more, it's exhausting. The psalmist knew crying out to God was the best defense against stress, and friend, it still works today. The next time you experience someone's wrath, take it right to God. Don't sit in it. Talk to the Lord. Tell Him everything, and then choose to trust He will work it out for your benefit and His glory.

#33

God Will Always Protect You

"When you pass through the deep, stormy sea, you can count on me to be there with you. When you pass through raging rivers, you will not drown. When you walk through persecution like fiery flames, you will not be burned; the flames will not harm you."

ISAIAH 43:2 TPT

This passage is why we don't have to give in to anxiety. God is clear when He tells us His game plan. It boils down to this: no matter what you're facing, no matter who is picking on you, no matter the guilt and shame that's stuck to you, no matter the number of people who dislike you, no matter the mess you've gotten yourself into, God will protect you. You won't drown in stress. You won't burn with worry. The Lord is with you, dear one. And because of that, you are saved.

#34

Assured Deliverance

I sought (inquired of) the Lord and required Him [of necessity and on the authority of His Word], and He heard me, and delivered me from all my fears.

PSALM 34:4 AMPC

Every time you cry out to the Lord, He hears you. No matter the circumstances weighing you down with worry, God knows what's going on. When all you can muster is a guttural noise through tears, He is fully aware of the situation that put you there. Make no mistake. Your Father's ear is always turned toward you, and it's because of His great love for you that God responds each time. The psalmist confirms that his deliverance came because of his prayers. He sought God in earnest and received complete liberation. This is fantastic news because it assures that when you ask the Lord for freedom from stress, worry, and anxiety, it will come.

Epic Stress Buster

Let the peace of Christ keep you in tune with each other, in step with each other. None of this going off and doing your own thing. And cultivate thankfulness. Let the Word of Christ—the Message—have the run of the house. Give it plenty of room in your lives. Instruct and direct one another using good common sense. And sing, sing your hearts out to God! Let every detail in your lives—words, actions, whatever—be done in the name of the Master, Jesus, thanking God the Father every step of the way.
COLOSSIANS 3:15–17 MSG

Want a stress buster? Take this passage of scripture to heart. It calls for community rather than handling problems alone. It suggests cultivating a thankful heart to see the silver lining. Make God's Word plus common sense a priority so your mind has no room to entertain worry. And choose joy at every turn. This focus will set you free from anxiety.

#36

Get to the Root

*"The heart is hopelessly dark and deceitful,
a puzzle that no one can figure out. But I, God, search
the heart and examine the mind. I get to the heart
of the human. I get to the root of things. I treat them
as they really are, not as they pretend to be."*
JEREMIAH 17:9–10 MSG

Remember that God knows you and the details of
your life. He knows what's stressing you out. He's
clear in His Word that He searches your heart
and examines your mind. Why? Because God has
a vested interest in your life. He makes a point to
keep His eyes on those He loves. You're important
to Him, and that's why the Lord keeps tabs on you,
friend. If there are worries, He cares. If there are
concerns, He listens. If there's anxiety, He relieves.
God is there for you and with you.

Quieting Your Heart

Quiet your heart in his presence and pray; keep hope alive as you long for God to come through for you. And don't think for a moment that the wicked in their prosperity are better off than you.

PSALM 37:7 TPT

When life feels chaotic and everything seems to be moving a mile a minute, ask the Lord to quiet your heart. Take a few deep breaths, step back from the craziness, and let God calm your anxious heart. Doing this offers perspective, something that's hard to grasp in the messy moments of life. It's also in His presence that your hope will be restored because you'll be reassured that He will come through for you. God won't ever leave you where you are. He is a God who promises to restore your heart to a state of peace if you'll ask. Tell the Lord what you need right now. He's listening!

When Stress Messes with Us

Let go of anger and leave rage behind! Don't get
upset—it will only lead to evil. Because evildoers
will be eliminated, but those who hope in
the LORD—they will possess the land.
PSALM 37:8–9 CEB

Stress messes with us. Not only are we weighed down with worry, we're also more easily angered because we don't have the normal bandwidth to deal with issues. We snap at those we care about most because we don't feel we have time to do what they're asking. We're impatient and cranky. Rather than cling to the hope that God will come through for us, we sit in the stress and become more agitated. But it doesn't have to be this way. The Lord will bring a calm to our heart when we ask. He will give us the ability to keep anxiety in check. Inviting Him into the situation gives us the reassurance we need to keep an eternal perspective, trusting peace is on its way.

Stress Is the Enemy

*Be strong! Be fearless! Don't be afraid and
don't be scared by your enemies, because the
LORD your God is the one who marches with you.
He won't let you down, and he won't abandon you.*
DEUTERONOMY 31:6 CEB

Stress is an enemy to your peace. It is designed to rob you of calm. Think of a time when bad news punched its way into your day, causing your heart to beat out of your chest. Remember how your mind raced as it was trying to process the information? Maybe you started sweating or crying. Regardless, harmony was hijacked. What if in those moments, you immediately started praying? In the next breath, you cried out to the Lord for help. This intentional decision to activate your faith has the potential to be a game-changer. It tells God you know He is more powerful than the enemy, and it unleashes His influence in your heart to restore the peace you once had.

#40

Sound Thoughts

*Those with sound thoughts you will keep
in peace, in peace because they trust in you.*
ISAIAH 26:3 CEB

As today's verse suggests, there is a very powerful connection between staying in peace and having sound thoughts. This is why we have to ask the Lord to help us control our thoughts. We have to be in charge of what thoughts get to land and which ones we don't allow, because if we don't monitor what we think, stress will take over and peace will be gone. We'll start thinking of horrible outcomes or endings. We'll feel judged or disliked. We'll let fear have its way and will start to partner with our insecurities. Rather than see a silver lining, we'll see a dark pit. Ask the Lord to keep your thoughts on good, positive things, and ask for God's help to keep your thoughts on His goodness in your life.

#41

Fasten Your Thoughts

*So keep your thoughts continually fixed on all
that is authentic and real, honorable and admirable,
beautiful and respectful, pure and holy, merciful
and kind. And fasten your thoughts on every glorious
work of God, praising him always. Follow the example
of all that we have imparted to you and the God
of peace will be with you in all things.*

<small>PHILIPPIANS 4:8–9 TPT</small>

With anxiety, your mind becomes a battlefield of
thoughts. If not careful, worry almost always takes
over, leaving you feeling overwhelmed and hopeless. You don't see a way out of the situation, and
rather than move on, you become trapped by those
negative thoughts in a spiral of negativity. Maybe
that's why these words from Philippians are so
important. They are a directive to navigate you
through stress and strife. Let things authentic, honorable, beautiful, and pure be what you fasten your
thoughts to every day.

#42

The Process of Maturing

I pray with great faith for you, because I'm fully convinced that the One who began this glorious work in you will faithfully continue the process of maturing you and will put his finishing touches to it until the unveiling of our Lord Jesus Christ!

PHILIPPIANS 1:6 TPT

Remember that you are in process. No matter what you do or how good of a student you are, your maturity will be complete in heaven. Your time on earth is all about growing in your faith. This is so vital to remember because it helps us realize that we won't do things perfectly here. You may know it's your faith in God that'll help manage stress, but there may be some days stress wins. Even your best effort won't always be enough. But God is patient and caring, and He will always be there when you need Him. Learn to embrace the maturing process as you keep trusting the Lord for peace and wisdom.

#43

The Relationship Between Stress and Fear

Love will never invoke fear. Perfect love expels fear, particularly the fear of punishment. The one who fears punishment has not been completed through love.
1 JOHN 4:18 VOICE

Few things evoke stress like fear. Being afraid heightens every sense and puts them all on alert. You become hypervigilant as you live and breathe in protection mode. And it becomes a hard cycle to break. The more you're afraid, the more you feel stress. The more you feel stress, the more fear rules in your heart. But the revelation of God's love expels fear. When you realize that you are loved and safe and secure in the Lord, it allows you to exhale. You're able to focus and make sense of what's causing you to feel overwhelmed. And your mind and body begin to realize they've been tricked, unaware of the toxic relationship between stress and fear. Friend, allow God's love to usher in a peaceful heart.

#44

Your Every Need

My God will meet your every need out of his riches in the glory that is found in Christ Jesus.
PHILIPPIANS 4:19 CEB

Friend, what do you need right now? Is it a way out of a stressful situation? Do you need peace to settle in your spirit? Do you need courage and confidence to put yourself out there again? Do you need to find a way to believe in your worth as a woman? Do you need a relationship to be restored? Think about it. What are you needing today? Whatever it is, you can breathe a sigh of relief because not only does the Lord know what you're battling, He also promises to meet your every need. He is able to bring peace. He can de-stress a situation. He will calm a heart. He can end your angst and worry. Today, talk to God about your immediate and pressing need for peace. And then rest, knowing He is working out the details.

#45

The Spirit Prays for You

A similar thing happens when we pray. We are weak and do not know how to pray, so the Spirit steps in and articulates prayers for us with groaning too profound for words. Don't you know that He who pursues and explores the human heart intimately knows the Spirit's mind because He pleads to God for His saints to align their lives with the will of God?
ROMANS 8:26–27 VOICE

Sometimes in our stress, we don't even know what to pray. We're not sure what we really need, so we stay silent. Our minds are taxed, and they shut down rather than cry out to God for help. But in His sovereignty, the Lord knew this was part of the human condition. That's why He assigned the Holy Spirit to intercede on your behalf. He is fully and completely aware of what's troubling you. So, when the words don't come. . .know the Spirit tells your needs directly to God for you.

Seeking the Kingdom

So do not consume yourselves with questions: What will we eat? What will we drink? What will we wear? Outsiders make themselves frantic over such questions; they don't realize that your heavenly Father knows exactly what you need. Seek first the kingdom of God and His righteousness, and then all these things will be given to you too.

MATTHEW 6:31–33 VOICE

Worrying often leads to asking yourself questions. You start thinking out loud about what could go wrong. You ask about the things that scare you, concerned about how it will all work out. *How will this work out? Will others be angry at me? Have I done something wrong? What do I do now?* You become frantic as you try to make the worry go away. You try to fix it yourself. But scripture says that if you'll seek the kingdom of God—seek the Lord's help—He will deliver a peace to your heart that'll melt the questions (and the worry) away.

#47

You Get to Choose

*Say to those who are panicking:
"Be strong! Don't fear! Here's your God,
coming with vengeance; with divine
retribution God will come to save you."*

ISAIAH 35:4 CEB

Let this be your challenge to stand up to the stress
that's trying to overtake you. So often, we choose to
partner with it. We let it rule our day and ruin our
mood as we give in to it. But you get to decide what
to do with it once it rears its ugly head. Will you entertain it, sitting in the worry it brings? Or will you
find the courage and confidence to take it right to
the One who can calm those joy-draining anxieties?
The Lord promises to right all the wrongs that are
keeping you stirred up. Your job is to choose to trust
Him no matter what.

Fortress of Protection

The Eternal is my light amidst my darkness and my
rescue in times of trouble. So whom shall I fear?
He surrounds me with a fortress of protection.
So nothing should cause me alarm.

PSALM 27:1 VOICE

What are the things that have happened this week to cause you alarm? A big fight with your husband? A screaming match with your kids? A surprise betrayal? A hurtful comment from a friend? Something on social media? A bad report at work? A new ache in your body? A bill you didn't see coming? Feeling insignificant? A moral failure on your part? No matter what it is, God is with you. Actually, you are lovingly surrounded by His unfailing protection. He's circling you because He loves you. God wants to be the One to help you work through the stress and strife. Remember, He is the light in the darkness that threatens to overtake you.

Your Kinsman-Redeemer

*Now, this is what Yahweh says: "Listen, Jacob,
to the One who created you, Israel, to the one
who shaped who you are. Do not fear, for I,
your Kinsman-Redeemer, will rescue you.
I have called you by name, and you are mine."*

Isaiah 43:1 TPT

God knows you. He knows your name. And He calls you to lean on Him when life feels overwhelming. Even more, God is your Kinsman-Redeemer, which means He lovingly assumes the responsibility of delivering you from the stress you're feeling. He is always ready to rescue His daughter from the situations causing strife. To Him, it's considered a privilege anytime you trust Him to redeem or vindicate on your behalf. The Father is protective of you, and He wants to lighten your load and heal your anxious heart. Talk to God right now about the circumstances that are troubling you. Tell Him about your worry. He's ready to help.

New Level of Trust

Jesus taught his disciples, saying, "Listen to me. Never let anxiety enter your hearts. Never worry about any of your needs, such as food or clothing. For your life is infinitely more than just food or the clothing you wear."
LUKE 12:22–23 TPT

Jesus was issuing a strong command to His disciples. Make sure you read today's verse through a lens of compassion rather than frustration. It was because of His deep love that He wanted to reassure His followers that their needs were known and would be met. He was offering them an eternal perspective, challenging them to a new level of trust. Friend, you're being called up too. Whatever is causing anxiety and worry in your life, have the faith to believe God is bigger. Know that your troubled heart hasn't escaped His eyes. Choose to trust that He is ready to intervene when you ask. Let the Lord into those anxious places.

The Strength to Stand

I look up to the mountains; does my strength come from mountains? No, my strength comes from GOD, who made heaven, and earth, and mountains.

PSALM 121:1–2 MSG

It's so important to know where your strength comes from. When you look to someone or something else to be your savior, you'll never find freedom. Too often, we choose to put our faith in earthly things, crossing our fingers that they will fix us. We hang our hope on people, money, alcohol, food, and the like to give us relief from anxious thoughts, but they leave us just as hopeless as before. The Lord wants to be the One to bring you peace, because He truly is the only One who can. God knows the false promises of the world. He understands your desire to want quick fixes. But in the end, God is where your strength to stand against the stress will come from.

#52

An Oasis of Peace

*He offers a resting place for me in his luxurious
love. His tracks take me to an oasis of peace,
the quiet brook of bliss. That's where he restores
and revives my life. He opens before me pathways to
God's pleasure and leads me along in his footsteps of
righteousness so that I can bring honor to his name.*

PSALM 23:2–3 TPT

What we need more than anything else when we're
stressed out is a place where we can find rest. Anxiety is exhausting because it keeps us stirred up.
Our emotions swirl like little tornados around our
mind and wear us out. Our heart aches. In those
moments, we're completely undone. It's almost unbearable. And while we crave peace, we just cannot
seem to find it or hold on to it. But friend, the Lord
has made a way to revive and restore us. Fall into
His arms, and let Him be your oasis of peace.

Help in the Unending Shadows

The Eternal is my shepherd, He cares for me always. . . . Even in the unending shadows of death's darkness, I am not overcome by fear. Because You are with me in those dark moments, near with Your protection and guidance, I am comforted.

PSALM 23:1, 4 VOICE

Anxiety can often be described as unending shadows. It can make you feel like something is hanging over you, casting darkness where there once was light and joy. Anxiety keeps happiness at bay because you're constantly being reminded of the weight stress and worry heap on your shoulders. But never forget that God is with you in those moments. It's His unshakable promise found throughout the Bible. He is there protecting you from the joy-draining seasons of life; and if you'll let Him, He will guide you through the valley of darkness into spacious places of peace.

Your Drooping Head

You serve me a six-course dinner right in front
of my enemies. You revive my drooping head;
my cup brims with blessing. Your beauty and
love chase after me every day of my life. I'm back
home in the house of God for the rest of my life.
PSALM 23:5–6 MSG

A drooping head may sound silly in today's verse,
but it's actually a great visual for how we often feel
when we're burdened with anxiety. Think about it.
Sometimes stress feels so heavy, we can barely lift
our head. We feel sluggish and tired. Our heart is
overwhelmed with emotions, and we just want to
climb into bed and disappear under the covers. But
what a relief to know that God is right there with us.
He's not worried about the difficult situations and
people in our life. Instead, He's blessing us right in
front of them. He has full authority over the anxiety
you're feeling. God's help brings hope every time.

#55

When You Feel Trapped

Fear and intimidation is a trap that holds you back.
But when you place your confidence in the Lord,
you will be seated in the high place.
PROVERBS 29:25 TPT

The only way we're going to get through life with
any measure of joy is to anchor our full trust in
God. There are so many things that come at us—
things we can't navigate well on our own—and we
need the Lord's help to walk them out with preci-
sion. There are seasons where it just seems to pile
on us at every turn. Between fear and intimidation, stress and worry, we're left feeling trapped in
hopelessness. The Lord sees you, friend. He understands what you're facing right now, and He's ready
to pull you from the mess and lift you high above it.
It doesn't mean you'll never feel stress again, but it
does guarantee you a way out when you do.

She Went to Jesus

*But Martha became exasperated by finishing
the numerous household chores in preparation
for her guests, so she interrupted Jesus and said,
"Lord, don't you think it's unfair that my sister
left me to do all the work by myself? You should
tell her to get up and help me."*
LUKE 10:40 TPT

Martha's story is a gift to women. God knew we'd need to read it, especially because it's still relevant. The stress that comes with preparing for and hosting people in our homes often tops the charts, and we're often overwhelmed with the anxiety of details. We're usually the ones stuck in the kitchen while others lounge and enjoy each other. In the end, we're frazzled and resentful. But notice how Martha went to the Lord with her frustration. That's the gold nugget. She knew He would make right what she felt was wrong. Remember, friend, you can do the same thing.

#57

Perception

The Lord answered her, "Martha, my beloved Martha. Why are you upset and troubled, pulled away by all these many distractions? Are they really that important? Mary has discovered the one thing most important by choosing to sit at my feet. She is undistracted, and I won't take this privilege from her."
LUKE 10:41–42 TPT

Yesterday, we applauded Martha for taking her frustrations to Jesus. Today, we're going to recognize the gift of a divine shift in perception. Stressed-out Martha was focused on the wrong things. From her kitchen, she was cooking up resentment for having to serve without help. But her moment with Jesus challenged her perspective. As women, we have the unique opportunity to bless friends and family in our homes. What if rather than letting our work cause anxiety and anger, we ask God to let peace reign in our hearts as we realize the privilege it is to love others well?

Already Defeated

Be aware that a time is coming when you will be scattered like seeds. You will return to your own way, and I will be left alone. But I will not be alone, because the Father will be with Me. I have told you these things so that you will be whole and at peace. In this world, you will be plagued with times of trouble, but you need not fear; I have triumphed over this corrupt world order.

JOHN 16:32–33 VOICE

In our anxiousness, we can feel alone. It may feel as though people have walked away, rejecting our pleas for help. Stress has a way of making you feel like an island, doesn't it? But the reality is you have a Father whose ear is trained on you. He never blinks or looks away. That's why we can find peace in uncertainty, because we believe He has our back. While God never promises an easy, stress-free life, He does promise the world won't win because He's already defeated it.

#59

A Sanctuary from Stress

He who takes refuge in the shelter of the Most High will be safe in the shadow of the Almighty. He will say to the Eternal, "My shelter, my mighty fortress, my God, I place all my trust in You."

PSALM 91:1–2 VOICE

Let God be your sanctuary from stress. When your marriage is in shambles or your child is being bullied, let the Lord be your refuge. When you're facing bankruptcy or the death of a loved one, He'll be your shelter. When the medical treatment isn't helping or your company announces layoffs, run to God for safety. At the end of the day, all we have is the Lord. And friend, that is enough! He is the One who can exchange every anxiety for peace. He won't leave you hopeless and worried about life. Instead, when you let Him be your sanctuary from stress, a sense of calm and confidence will saturate your heart.

#60

Bringing You the Victory

You will never worry about an attack of demonic forces at night nor have to fear a spirit of darkness coming against you. Don't fear a thing! Whether by night or by day, demonic danger will not trouble you, nor will the powers of evil launched against you.

PSALM 91:5–6 TPT

One way the enemy likes to discourage you is through anxious thoughts. He makes you look down the road to see horrible outcomes and endings to situations where you're already worried. He breeds fear in your heart, making you terrified your husband will leave, your children will be unsuccessful, your treatment plan will fail, or a million other ways your life will end badly. But God has made a way for you to see clearly through these attacks. Every time worry and stress creep into your heart, tell Him what's stirring in you. He won't leave you to fight alone. Instead, it's the Lord who will bring you the victory over any demonic plan.

#61

You're Being Watched

God sends angels with special orders to protect you wherever you go, defending you from all harm. If you walk into a trap, they'll be there for you and keep you from stumbling. You'll even walk unharmed among the fiercest powers of darkness, trampling every one of them beneath your feet!
PSALM 91:11–13 TPT

Scripture says the Lord has given angels special orders to protect you. Wherever you go, they're commanded to defend you. Can you even imagine? Think of all the stress-inducing situations they've kept you from. Imagine the anxiety-ridden moments you've been spared because these angels followed God's orders. While we've all had our fair share of worrisome moments, what a gift to know there have been many we were protected from. You've not experienced all the enemy had planned—not by a long shot. And you can trust the stressful situations you did face were allowed only for your benefit and His glory. What an amazing Father!

Times of Pressure and Trouble

"I will answer your cry for help every time you pray, and you will find and feel my presence even in your time of pressure and trouble. I will be your glorious hero and give you a feast. You will be satisfied with a full life and with all that I do for you. For you will enjoy the fullness of my salvation!"

PSALM 91:15–16 TPT

What an amazing revelation confirmed by this verse. If you've ever wondered if your prayers were heard by God, here's compelling truth they are indeed. As a matter of fact, the passage says He answers you every single time you pray, even in times of pressure and trouble. How does this truth land in your heart today? Maybe you're struggling with stressful situations at home or at work. Maybe you're suffering from anxiety as you navigate personal trauma. Hold tight to the promise that God hears you and is working on your behalf right now.

Compassion for the Brokenhearted

*For the Eternal watches over the righteous,
and His ears are attuned to their prayers. He is
always listening. . . . When the upright need help
and cry to the Eternal, He hears their cries and
rescues them from all of their troubles. When
someone is hurting or brokenhearted, the Eternal
moves in close and revives him in his pain.*

PSALM 34:15, 17–18 VOICE

God's heart is so tender toward those who are hurting or brokenhearted. He understands that this life has a way of beating us up. He knows the struggles and battles we will be facing. And the Lord is aware of the anxiety our bodies, hearts, and minds will experience in our lifetime. What a gift to have such a compassionate God who cares so deeply and watches over you. What a blessing to know He is always listening for your voice, waiting to rescue you when you cry out. You're never alone.

#64

Relational Stress

If you love life and want to live a good, long time, take care with the things you say. Don't lie or spread gossip or talk about improper things. Walk away from the evil things of the world, and always seek peace and pursue it.

PSALM 34:12–14 VOICE

It's so hard to be at odds with others. Most of us want to live a peaceful life and get along with those around us. We crave harmony. So, when we find ourselves fighting and arguing, it creates stress. But God reminds us how to be a blessing to our community, and it has to do with watching our words. Be careful with what you say. Avoid any temptation to use your words in negative ways. It's just not worth it. Once you say something, it's not retractable; and eventually the anxiety over what you said overwhelms. So, choose to bless and not curse, and live in peace.

#65

The Power of Praise to Battle Anxiety

I will praise the Eternal in every moment through every situation. Whenever I speak, my words will always praise Him. Everything within me wants to pay tribute to Him. Whenever the poor and humble hear of His greatness, they will celebrate too! Come and lift up the Eternal with me; let's praise His name together!

PSALM 34:1–3 VOICE

If you stay busy praising the Lord in every situation, in every struggle, and in every stressor, you won't have time to focus on your troubles. Not only that, but it will bolster your faith that God is in control and will bring you to the other side of worry and fear. Try it. The next time anxiety begins to grow, start thanking God. When worry pops up, begin to recount all the ways He's been faithful. Instead of partnering with fear, think of times the Lord saved or protected you. Never forget that praise is a powerful weapon against anxiety.

#66

Wipe Your Tears

"He will wipe away every tear from their eyes. Death will be no more. There will be no mourning, crying, or pain anymore, for the former things have passed away."
REVELATION 21:4 CEB

Does stress ever reduce you to a puddle of tears? Sometimes those overwhelming feelings leak out of our eyes as we try to make sense of what we're feeling. It's hard to stay cool, calm, and collected when our hearts are hurting. We can't always be composed when we're anxious about what's coming next. And worry and fear do nothing but agitate us because our emotions are raw and stirred up. But isn't it just like God to promise us that He'll wipe every tear away? It's such an encouragement to know that we won't always have wet cheeks from crying. Anxiety won't always win. And one day, we'll stand stress-free in the Father's presence, and it will be glorious.

Press in for Peace

*Now may the Lord of peace Himself grant
you His peace at all times and in every way
[that peace and spiritual well-being that comes
to those who walk with Him, regardless of life's
circumstances]. The Lord be with you all.*

2 Thessalonians 3:16 AMP

Do you think it's possible to have peace at all times
and in every way? Living without stress and strife
sometimes feels like a pie-in-the-sky dream. We
look at those around us, our circumstances, and
our own heart and decide this is too far off for us.
But Paul tells us in his letter to the church that it is
possible if God grants it to you. It comes from Him.
Why would He do that? Consider it a blessing for
choosing a righteous life. When you press into the
Lord when life presses in on you, He will give you
His peace.

#68

The Invitation to Investigate

Investigate my life, O God, find out everything about me; cross-examine and test me, get a clear picture of what I'm about; see for yourself whether I've done anything wrong—then guide me on the road to eternal life.

PSALM 139:23–24 MSG

What if you tasked the Lord with investigating your life, looking for pockets of stress? What if you invited Him to find and expose the areas where anxiety hides? Only God can completely heal our insecurities. He is the One who can bring restoration to those broken places inside. Unless we surrender to the Lord, we will continue to battle those stressors without experiencing His peace. Spend time today talking to God about the idea of being so vulnerable with Him. Let Him know what keeps you from inviting His investigation. Ask the Lord to build your confidence and courage to let Him heal you from the inside out.

He Always Knows

Where could I go from your Spirit? Where could I run and hide from your face? If I go up to heaven, you're there! If I go down to the realm of the dead, you're there too! If I fly with wings into the shining dawn, you're there! If I fly into the radiant sunset, you're there waiting! Wherever I go, your hand will guide me; your strength will empower me.

PSALM 139:7–10 TPT

God always knows. He sees the tears you cry in your marriage. He knows the ways your mama-heart breaks from time to time. He hears your negative self-talk as you recount the stressors of the day. He sees the ways you're let down and the heartache that comes with it. He is aware of those anxious thoughts that plague you in the night. And because He knows, He promises to give you the strength and courage to navigate them with power and peace.

Every Single Moment

Every single moment you are thinking of me!
How precious and wonderful to consider that
you cherish me constantly in your every thought!
O God, your desires toward me are more than
the grains of sand on every shore! When I awake
each morning, you're still with me.
PSALM 139:17–18 TPT

You may not feel cherished by anyone in your family. You may be short of friends right now. Maybe you don't feel like you really matter to those around you. And it might seem like no one cares if you're stressed out or struggling in life. But friend, that's not how God feels. Not at all. Scripture says that He is thinking of you every single moment. Isn't that mind-boggling? Not a second goes by that you don't cross His mind. So, while you may agonize, worried no one cares, rest knowing that God does and He always will. You matter greatly to God!

#71

Surrender Your Anxiety

Surrender your anxiety! Be silent and stop your striving and you will see that I am God. I am the God above all the nations, and I will be exalted throughout the whole earth.

PSALM 46:10 TPT

When you surrender your anxiety, it means you're giving up control. Sometimes we hold on to anxiety because it gives us permission to be messy. We have an excuse for our behavior. It becomes a part of our identity, and we learn to milk it for attention. So, the idea of healing from anxiousness and finding peace feels too risky. But friend, you weren't created to thrive in stress. It's not healthy for mind or body. Instead, you were made to live with joy and peace. God wants this for you! When you surrender your anxiety, setting your striving tendencies aside, it frees Him up to do some deep work in your heart. And that will free you to enjoy life!

#72

Waiting on God

But those who trust in the Eternal One will regain their strength. They will soar on wings as eagles. They will run—never winded, never weary. They will walk—never tired, never faint.

ISAIAH 40:31 VOICE

Sometimes the hardest thing to do is wait on God, especially when you're desperate for help. You want Him to intervene right then and there. You need His answer yesterday. And when you're in a stressful situation in need of relief, patiently waiting seems almost unbearable. This is where the rubber meets the road with your faith. This is when your belief in the Lord's faithfulness must be steadfast. When you choose to place your trust in Him, you will find the strength necessary to continue. You will find perseverance. You will have endurance. You'll be able to navigate the anxiety-inducing situations as you wait for God's help. Trust His timing and plan. He's never late.

Choosing a Joyful Heart

A joyful, cheerful heart brings healing to both body and soul. But the one whose heart is crushed struggles with sickness and depression.
PROVERBS 17:22 TPT

What if—when the stress hit—you chose to be joyful instead? What if you refused to partner with anxiety? The truth is that you have a choice. While your first reaction may be to freak out at bad news, let your second response be joy. You can't always contain those initial reactions, but you can most certainly choose what comes next. Stressful situations are a part of life, but if you're always giving in to them, scripture says your heart will become sick. That's hopelessness. And friend, that's no way to live your one and only life. You can have joy because of God's assurance that He is faithful to save you. He promises to restore a broken and stressed-out heart. And even more, He reminds you He'll never leave you to handle life on your own.

Experience Joy

My fellow believers, when it seems as though you are facing nothing but difficulties see it as an invaluable opportunity to experience the greatest joy that you can! For you know that when your faith is tested it stirs up power within you to endure all things. And then as your endurance grows even stronger it will release perfection into every part of your being until there is nothing missing and nothing lacking.

JAMES 1:2–4 TPT

Few would argue that stress tests your faith. Sometimes it takes all you have to trust God when your heart is freaking out with fear. It's not easy to hold on to hope when your anxious thoughts are all-consuming. When you are weighted down with worry, choosing to find joy seems impossible. But if you ask the Lord to increase your faith and endurance in Him and His timing, you'll receive a shift in perspective. That perspective will enable you to find joy and peace through the moments of stress and strife.

#75

The Trials of Life

Happy is the person who can hold up under the trials of life. At the right time, he'll know God's sweet approval and will be crowned with life. As God has promised, the crown awaits all who love Him.
JAMES 1:12 VOICE

James tells us if we can stay strong throughout the trials of life, we'll find happiness. We can't allow ourselves to crumble under the weight of worry. Although we may feel it, we can't let it press us down into discouragement. It means we don't let stressful situations have dominion over our sanity. We keep a positive outlook because we know God is working. We don't let angst and anxiety rule our day, dictating our mood and how we treat those around us. Instead, stand your ground. Lean into God's faithfulness. Choose to believe He is actively involved to deliver you.

#76

Always a Priority

Here is the bottom line: do not worry about your life. Don't worry about what you will eat or what you will drink. Don't worry about how you clothe your body. Living is about more than merely eating, and the body is about more than dressing up.

MATTHEW 6:25 VOICE

How easy it is to say we should not worry, but walking it out as a rule of thumb is so much harder. Amen? For many, worry is just part of their day. It's not even a conscious decision but rather a default button. But the Lord wants you to know that He has your best in mind at all times. No matter what worry crosses your mind, you can be assured He's already working on it. God has made provision where it's needed. He's planned for healing and restoration. God has gone before you to clear the path ahead, and He offers you rest when you embrace the truth that you're always a priority to Him.

Better Than Birds

Look at the birds in the sky. They do not store food for winter. They don't plant gardens. They do not sow or reap—and yet, they are always fed because your heavenly Father feeds them. And you are even more precious to Him than a beautiful bird. If He looks after them, of course He will look after you.
MATTHEW 6:26 VOICE

Sometimes we need a shift in perspective to better understand how much God loves us and will meet our needs. It's easy to get lost in our anxious thoughts and be afraid how the future might turn out. We worry about the variables. We stress about the details. But the Lord invites you to think about the birds, who always have what they need to survive. Somehow, these birds are able to find food and shelter and thrive no matter the conditions they face. Friend, if God considers you more precious than the birds He provides for, why waste any time sitting in anxiety about how He will take care of you? God sees you and knows your needs. Trust Him.

Worry Adds Nothing Good

*"So, which one of you by worrying
could add anything to your life?"*
MATTHEW 6:27 TPT

Worrying adds nothing good to your life. Think about it. When you worry, it doesn't add hope. It doesn't add excitement for what's to come. Worrying doesn't increase your faith or encourage you to have peace. It has never added any level of comfort to your situation. Worry doesn't make you sleep any better, does it? No. Worry only takes away from what God wants for you. It robs you of the blessings that come from waiting. It steals harmony and productivity, and it keeps your emotions stirred up. When stress starts to rise in your heart, go right to God with it. Let Him take it away so you can stand strong in faith regardless of what comes your way.

#79

Thank God Now

*"And why would you worry about your clothing?
Look at all the beautiful flowers of the field. They
don't work or toil, and yet not even Solomon in all
his splendor was robed in beauty more than one of
these! So if God has clothed the meadow with hay,
which is here for such a short time and then dried up
and burned, won't he provide for you the clothes you
need—even though you live with such little faith?"*
MATTHEW 6:28–30 TPT

It's human nature to worry about provision. We
worry about how we'll pay the bills, how we'll fill
the pantry or the kids' closets, and about the financial strain of our years of retirement. Life can change
on a dime, and we've learned the hard way there's
no sure thing on earth. But God never changes and
neither do His promises to provide. Rather than
spend another moment entertaining that age-old
anxiety, why not begin to thank God now for all the
ways He's already made a way? With Him, there is
no need to worry at all.

#80

Relax

*"What I'm trying to do here is to get you to relax,
to not be so preoccupied with getting, so you can
respond to God's giving. People who don't know God
and the way he works fuss over these things, but you
know both God and how he works. Steep your life in
God-reality, God-initiative, God-provisions. Don't
worry about missing out. You'll find all your
everyday human concerns will be met."*

MATTHEW 6:31–33 MSG

Take a deep breath, friend. Exhale your preoccupation with getting your needs met. Release the tension of trying to control and manipulate the outcomes of the things that scare you. Let go of the expectations that are keeping you in bondage. God's message to you in this moment is to relax and choose to believe God sees your every need. Even more, He will meet them at the right time and in the right ways. His future for you is full of hope and goodness. Choose this day to trust!

Surrendering Fear

"Don't worry or surrender to your fear.
For you've believed in God, now trust
and believe in me also."

JOHN 14:1 TPT

Fear is something we all deal with from time to time. It has a way of rattling us to the bone if we let it. It can disable us and cause us to doubt that good things are possible. Fear tells us everything will end up badly so why try for a different outcome. It has the ability to rock our very foundation and undo the healing we've worked so hard for. This is exactly why God's Word says to surrender your fear and trust God. You weren't built to carry the worry that comes with life. His plan all along was to be the One to take it from you. Fear is inevitable, but what you do with it can either lead to peace or an anxious heart.

#82

God of Possibilities

*For with God nothing is ever impossible
and no word from God shall be without
power or impossible of fulfillment.*
LUKE 1:37 AMPC

Sweet one, it's time to loosen the grip you have on stress. It might feel like you're at a dead end, but you simply are not. It may seem like it will never work out, but God is at work. You might think making ends meet is up to you alone, but scripture doesn't back that up. Before you lose all hope, cry out to the Lord for His help. The truth is that what looks impossible right now can be deceiving. The enemy's plan is for you to end up discouraged. But God is quick to remind through His Word that He is the God of possibilities. Impossible isn't in His vocabulary. So, when you get to the end of yourself, reach out to the Lord for exactly what you need.

#83

Let Him Embolden You!

Have not I commanded you? Be strong,
vigorous, and very courageous. Be not afraid,
neither be dismayed, for the Lord your God
is with you wherever you go.

JOSHUA 1:9 AMPC

You don't have to live in defeat. Your past sins don't relegate you to a life of hopelessness. You're not being punished for being imperfect, and you don't have to walk around carrying shame and guilt any longer. Those ways of living breed anxiety and fear. Instead, God is clear in His command when He says to be strong and full of courage. Do you know why He can ask that of you, especially knowing the pitfalls of this world? It's because the plan is for Him to be with you always. No matter where you go, God is there. So when you hit the wall of anxiety, find the peace you crave by surrendering stress to Him, and ask Him to embolden you to continue!

#84

A Ball of Stress

Which one of you can add a single hour
to your life or 18 inches to your height
by worrying really hard?
LUKE 12:25 VOICE

Can worry make your marriage better? Can it help undo the financial strain you're under? Does worrying help your kids perform better at school or on the court? Does it make your health improve? When you let worry rule in your heart, does it encourage kindness and gentleness? Can it change your day for the better? No, friend. Stress and anxiety do nothing but remove your peace and dismantle your mood. And the Lord wants none of that for you. It's hard to be effective in our relationships when we're a ball of stress. Let the Lord into your mess and ask for His help and strength. Your hope lies in Him and Him alone.

Firmly Rooted in Truth

*But blessed is the one who trusts in Me alone;
the Eternal will be his confidence. He is like a
tree planted by water, sending out its roots beside
the stream. It does not fear the heat or even drought.
Its leaves stay green and its fruit is dependable,
no matter what it faces.*
JEREMIAH 17:7–8 VOICE

When you spend time in the Word and regularly connect with God, your investment pays off. The fruit that comes from your pursuit of the Lord deepens your faith and dependence on Him. The depth of commitment strengthens you for the hard seasons you're going to weather, even if you aren't in one right now. So when the storms come rolling in, along with all the anxiety and stress, you won't be moved. You may be shaken for a time, but you will remain firmly rooted in the truth that God is trustworthy and faithful, and that's why you can be confident.

#86

Where We Slip Up

*The minute I said, "I'm slipping, I'm falling,"
your love, G$_{OD}$, took hold and held me fast.
When I was upset and beside myself, you
calmed me down and cheered me up.*

PSALM 94:18–19 MSG

It seems there are too many places we can slip up these days. From parenting out of anger to missing important deadlines at work. From entertaining situations that might cause a moral failure to threatening divorce as a way to manipulate. We've made countless wrong choices and worried about the natural consequences. And chances are a decision has landed us in the doghouse a time or two, leaving us emotionally distraught and discouraged. Next time, invite God into your pain. He never expects perfection, and when you ask, His love will calm your anxious heart in powerful and necessary ways.

How to Let Peace Reign

*You will guard him and keep him in perfect
and constant peace whose mind [both its
inclination and its character] is stayed on You,
because he commits himself to You, leans
on You, and hopes confidently in You.*

ISAIAH 26:3 AMPC

Where do you need peace right now? Is there a relationship that's destabilizing? Are you worried about a doctor's report? Does the move look hopeless? Is a child rocking your home with their terrible decisions? Are your finances a mess? Did you get overlooked for the promotion again? God's Word says that when you choose to keep focused on Him and trust that He's active and present in your situation, you can and will experience peace. Right there in the middle of your mess, the peace of Jesus will reign in your heart and rule in your life. Commit today to lean on God, and place all your hope in Him!

#88

He's Got You

*"That's right. Because I, your God, have a firm grip
on you and I'm not letting go. I'm telling you,
'Don't panic. I'm right here to help you.'"*
Isaiah 41:13 msg

It's important to remember that God won't ever let go of you although others might. You may have a relationship or two come to an end that you never saw coming. You'll lose people you deeply care about to death. Many will move across town or to another part of the country, and your bond will naturally deteriorate. And some might have to use their time and effort elsewhere, in areas that require more of them now than before. It's normal for our tribe to change as we go through life. But the one constant who will always be your sounding board and encourager through stress and strife will be the Lord. And friend, His grip on you is firm and loving. Tell Him what you need!

#89

Count on God

"Count on it: Everyone who had it in for you will end up out in the cold—real losers. Those who worked against you will end up empty-handed—nothing to show for their lives. When you go out looking for your old adversaries you won't find them—not a trace of your old enemies, not even a memory."
ISAIAH 41:11–12 MSG

Don't worry. The Lord knows your frustration. He has seen every situation where people tried to hurt you. He saw the ones who worked against you and brought so much stress into your life. He is fully aware of the times where your best interest wasn't considered. None of the rude, mean-spirited, hateful comments sneaked past the Lord. And rest assured He has been with you through it all. You weren't alone, and you weren't expected to navigate those stress-filled situations on your own. Count on God to be with you always. His heart is for you and will not let you fall into the pit of despair. He'll take care of you every step of the way.

#90

Compassion Fatigue Remedy

So let's not allow ourselves to get fatigued doing good. At the right time we will harvest a good crop if we don't give up, or quit. Right now, therefore, every time we get the chance, let us work for the benefit of all, starting with the people closest to us in the community of faith.

GALATIANS 6:9–10 MSG

It's common to grow tired from helping others. It's called *compassion fatigue*, and it's a real thing we all battle. Along with tiredness can come stress from trying to be everything to everyone. Our heart may be in the right place, but we reach our human limitations when we're working in our own strength rather than asking God to give us His strength. Be it helping your kids navigate the divorce to taking care of your aging parents to volunteering at the homeless shelter, we need the Lord to fortify and support our efforts. Make sure He is your go-to for energy and focus and stamina. It will help alleviate the anxiety that comes with the territory.

Company Stress

Oh Martha, Martha, you are so anxious and concerned about a million details, but really, only one thing matters. Mary has chosen that one thing, and I won't take it away from her.
LUKE 10:41–42 VOICE

Poor Martha was a mess. She was trying to make her home as comfortable and inviting as possible for Jesus and company. Rather than enjoy the preparations, she was anxious. Can you relate? Company stress is a stress all to itself. It's as if our identity is wrapped up in the state of our home and our culinary skills. And the gold nugget from today's scripture is that Martha went right to Jesus with her frustration. Rather than stew in stress and anxiety, she asked Jesus for help. His answer may not have been what she wanted to hear, but it was truth to hang her hat on. And it was said in love. You'll get the same responses when you take your frustrations to the Lord.

#92

Asking for Help

*But in the day that I'm afraid, I lay all
my fears before you and trust in
you with all my heart.*

PSALM 56:3 TPT

Sometimes it's hard to accept help because it feels like you're weak or unable to handle life on your own. But the truth is that being self-sufficient was never part of God's plan for you. He simply didn't design you to go rogue. You weren't created to be a solo act. And anxiety often pops up in those moments where we have to ask for support—be it from a friend or family member or even God. But if you want to conquer the anxiety you're feeling, the Lord invites you to lay every fear and worry before Him. Accept His offer to help you navigate those tough moments, trusting that He will calm your anxious heart and give you hope.

When Life Slaps You Hopeless

*"In this godless world you will continue
to experience difficulties. But take heart!
I've conquered the world."*
JOHN 16:33 MSG

A sense of hopelessness is hard to overcome when it feels like life is slapping you at every turn. It can feel as if you'll never catch a break from the discouragement and difficulties. From friendship frustration to financial freak-outs to future fears, it's easy to want to throw in the towel and give up. But the Lord is clear that we're to expect the kind of situations that can stir up anxiety. The Word tells us that life will be challenging. But when you choose to press into Him with every anxious moment and invite Him into the stress and fear that plague you, He will provide a sense of peace and a divine perspective that will calm every worry you're facing.

#94

Expect Messy Seasons

Lord, even when your path takes me through the valley of deepest darkness, fear will never conquer me, for you already have! You remain close to me and lead me through it all the way. Your authority is my strength and my peace. The comfort of your love takes away my fear. I'll never be lonely, for you are near.

PSALM 23:4 TPT

We must learn to expect messy seasons that can threaten us with worry and anxiety. Life ebbs and flows with high and low moments. To expect smooth sailing sets us up for huge disappointments. It's just not realistic to expect mountaintop experiences every day. But here's what we can cling to during the deep, dark valley times—God's guidance and comfort. The Lord will be right with you, and His presence will calm the anxiety as you trust Him. Those tough seasons are a normal part of life; that's why the Lord promises to stay close.

Never Give Up Hope

May the God of your hope so fill you with all joy and peace in believing [through the experience of your faith] that by the power of the Holy Spirit you may abound and be overflowing (bubbling over) with hope.

ROMANS 15:13 AMPC

In those moments when it feels like the world is coming apart, cry out to the Lord. When everything that could go wrong does go wrong, share your fearful heart with God. When your stress and anxiety are off the charts and you can't find hope, pray for it. The Lord always honors your choice to trust Him. He hears every prayer you send His way and will always respond at the right time and in the right way for your situation. No matter what you're dealing with, His Spirit will allow you to bubble over with hope!

#96

Unshakable Peace

*The fundamental fact of existence is that
this trust in God, this faith, is the firm foundation
under everything that makes life worth living. It's our
handle on what we can't see. The act of faith is what
distinguished our ancestors, set them above the crowd.*
HEBREWS 11:1–2 MSG

If you make your faith in God the foundation of every part of your life, you will have unshakable peace. It's an act of surrender to make the choice to trust the Lord over your own abilities. It's choosing to believe God more than your closest, wisest friend. It's deciding that regardless of the difficult life that's staring you down, you will always place your faith in Him. If you can embrace this shift in living, anxiety and fear and insecurities won't have power over you any longer. Instead, you will choose faith over fear at every turn.

Taming Anxious Thoughts

So what should we say about all of this?
If God is on our side, then tell me:
whom should we fear?
ROMANS 8:31 VOICE

When something concerns you, does your mind start down a rabbit hole of anxious thoughts? Rather than thinking positive thoughts, do you often predict horrible outcomes and endings without hope for good to win? Do you decide everything will fail, so there's no point in trying? It can be difficult to be confident when life continues to be hard. Being optimistic in the face of hardship so often feels undoable. That's why today's verse is so important for us to remember! It gives hope to the weary, and it reminds us to leave anxious thoughts at the Lord's feet because fear doesn't win when God's involved. With Him on our side, those anxious thoughts are tamed.

#98

Making Peace with Do-Overs

Don't let even one rotten word seep out of your mouths. Instead, offer only fresh words that build others up when they need it most. That way your good words will communicate grace to those who hear them.

EPHESIANS 4:29 VOICE

So much anxiety comes from our rotten treatment of others. When we say hurtful words or respond in anger, when we treat someone as unimportant, when our actions tell others they're an inconvenience, eventually our conscience catches up and we feel terrible. In those moments, remember that God's grace is available. You can confess your bad choices, ask for forgiveness, and receive a clean slate. You don't have to beat yourself up over and over again. With God, you can make peace with do-overs as you reconnect with those you've hurt. You can be the kind of woman to offer fresh, kind words.

#99

His Perfect Plan of Goodness

So we are convinced that every detail of our lives is continually woven together to fit into God's perfect plan of bringing good into our lives, for we are his lovers who have been called to fulfill his designed purpose.

ROMANS 8:28 TPT

Why worry about your life, especially after reading the truth bomb in today's verse. If God works every detail of your life together to fit into His plan, that means nothing is by chance. There are no accidents. Nothing has escaped the Lord's eye. There's nothing to be anxious about when you realize that God is in full control no matter what. And His hand in your life is continual. It's not a once-and-done moment in time. Instead, God is intimately engaged to bring beauty from ashes. So, when you begin to stress out and fill with anxiety, remember that He is right there with you, working His perfect plan of goodness.

#100

Never Quit on You

When I walk into the thick of trouble, keep me alive in the angry turmoil. With one hand strike my foes, with your other hand save me. Finish what you started in me, God. Your love is eternal—don't quit on me now.

PSALM 138:7–8 MSG

In those heartbreaking moments when those you've trusted the most have given up on you, remember that God never will. He is faithful without fail because His love for you is eternal. It's unchanging. It's unshakable. And while you're left to battle the anxiety from a friend or family member's rejection or abandonment, you can always count on the Lord's commitment to you. You can rest knowing He will complete His good work in your life. And you will find comfort and peace to trump the loneliness you're feeling. Life will bring stressors of all kinds, but God will calm your anxious heart with His love.

#101

Your Portal to Power

So I'm not defeated by my weakness,
but delighted! For when I feel my weakness and
endure mistreatment—when I'm surrounded with
troubles on every side and face persecution because
of my love for Christ—I am made yet stronger. For
my weakness becomes a portal to God's power.
2 CORINTHIANS 12:10 TPT

Sometimes weakness amplifies our insecurities, making us feel insignificant and pathetic because we're sure we'll never have the strength we need. We worry we'll live a life of failure. We obsess we won't accomplish important and necessary things. And that stress sits on our shoulders, weighing us down. But what if you looked at it through the lens of faith and realized that weakness is a portal to God's power in you. When you access that power, it'll make you stronger and able to manage the stress and strife that come your way. Admitting your weakness to the Lord invites His power to course through your veins, giving you the supernatural ability to thrive.

Keeping Your Head above Water

And He will be leading you. He'll be with you, and He'll never fail you or abandon you. So don't be afraid!
DEUTERONOMY 31:8 VOICE

When anxiety is at its greatest, there is no lonelier feeling in the world. It has a special way of making you feel isolated, like no one understands what you're going through. It gives you tunnel vision so that all you focus on are the things that stress you out. You worry that all will implode, so your brain works overtime trying to fix the issues. But why not ask God to help? What keeps you from crying out to Him for courage and confidence? Why not look to Him for solutions and answers? Why not ask for His peace? It's so vital to remember there is nothing that can separate you from the Lord. He's a constant in your life. And when anxiety feels like it's pulling you underwater, God promises to keep your head above it. Stress is not your friend, and it serves no good purpose. Let the Lord take it from you as He comforts you with His presence.

#103

More Than Enough Grace

*God has the power to provide you with more
than enough of every kind of grace. That way,
you will have everything you need always and
in everything to provide more than enough
for every kind of good work.*
2 Corinthians 9:8 ceb

One of the reasons we stress out is because we lack
the grace to let things go. We hold on to the rude
comment from our husband as he left for work.
We remember the way we were talked to by our
boss in the middle of the meeting. We can recall
that snarky response from the kids when we asked
them to help around the house. And when we collect these offenses, they pile up in our heart and
cause anxiety. Have you ever asked the Lord to
give you more grace. . .or the right kind of grace?
He's ready to supply you with whatever you need
when you ask, and His grace can remove the stress
buildup weighing you down.

#104

To Save and Rescue

For this is how much God loved the world—
he gave his one and only, unique Son as a gift.
So now everyone who believes in him will never
perish but experience everlasting life. "God did not
send his Son into the world to judge and condemn
the world, but to be its Savior and rescue it!"
JOHN 3:16–17 TPT

Do you ever worry about coming face-to-face with God, stressed out by the condemnation you feel will be coming your way? It can be overwhelming to think of all we've done that we know offends the Lord. It's easy to be timid with Him because we are certain He is angry or disappointed in some of the choices we've made. We are sure our decisions have been a source of frustration for God. So, we hide from Him rather than invite Him into the anxiety that keeps us awake at night. But Jesus—because of God's great love—came to save and rescue you, not to judge and condemn. Ask Him to remove that unfounded stress so nothing will hinder your relationship. Trust His heart for you.

#105

Be the Encourager

Energize the limp hands, strengthen the rubbery knees. Tell fearful souls, "Courage! Take heart! God is here, right here, on his way to put things right and redress all wrongs. He's on his way! He'll save you!"
ISAIAH 35:3–4 MSG

One of the best ways we can love others is to be a constant and powerful reminder that God is with them and always active in their stressful situation. We can be an encourager to the disheartened, pointing them to the Lord for hope and help. Although this truth sounds like a no-brainer, stress often makes us forget what we normally know is right and good. We get tangled by lies from the enemy. Our mind becomes a battlefield, and too often anxiety wins out. So watch for opportunities to remind those you care about that God will equip them to walk through their stressful circumstances with confidence and courage. We all need reassurance in those tough seasons of life.

#106

When We Can't Find the Words

"So when they put you under arrest and hand you over for trial, don't even give one thought about what you will say. Simply speak what the Holy Spirit gives you at that very moment. And realize that it won't be you speaking but the Holy Spirit repeatedly speaking through you."

MARK 13:11 TPT

Sometimes stress makes us tongue-tied, and we struggle to express what we're really feeling. We can't find the words to unpack our anxious heart, so we suffer in silence. We try to handle it all alone because it just feels easier. We try to make sense of the worry we're experiencing, but the weight of it is overwhelming. When we can't find the words, we can trust that the Holy Spirit will give them to us. He has absolute knowledge of what we're feeling. He sees the minute details of our anxiousness. And He'll help us find the right words to share at the right time with God and others about our struggle with stress.

God Doesn't Tempt

When you are tempted don't ever say, "God is tempting me," for God is incapable of being tempted by evil and he is never the source of temptation.

JAMES 1:13 TPT

The Word says to never point a finger at God, declaring that He is the source of temptation. The simple yet powerful truth is that He is incapable and unwilling to tempt you. You may face trials in life when He's teaching you important truths, but He would never tempt you to sin or make bad choices. It's not in His flawless character. So, when you're feeling stressed or afraid, ask Him for clarity. Ask if the issue causing anxiety is a lesson He wants you to learn, like giving up control or living unoffended. Or ask if the enemy is tempting you with fear or worry to get you to step out of God's will for your life. It's critical to know the difference, and if you ask God, He'll let you know.

#108

Listen and Love

My dearest brothers and sisters, take this to heart:
Be quick to listen, but slow to speak. And be slow to
become angry, for human anger is never a legitimate
tool to promote God's righteous purpose.
JAMES 1:19–20 TPT

Anxiety often makes us act out of character. Although you're normally a kind and gentle soul, stress can cause you to say hurtful things. Rather than look for opportunities to bless others, you focus on yourself. An anxious heart can cause you to be careless with the needs of others. That's why today's verse is so important, because it reminds you to do a self-check. Think about it. Is stress getting the best of you, making you quick to anger? Are you listening to others or purging everything on your mind? Is fear and worry making you cranky and unloving toward others? If so, ask God to replace stress with peace so you can love your community well.

#109

Not an Inconvenience

For God has proved his love by giving us his greatest treasure, the gift of his Son. And since God freely offered him up as the sacrifice for us all, he certainly won't withhold from us anything else he has to give.
ROMANS 8:32 TPT

Friend, you're not an inconvenience. I know it may feel that way at times, especially when our requests seem to annoy those around us. But you're never an inconvenience to God. Just think about it. If God willingly gave His Son to die on the cross with the sole purpose of bridging the gap between you and Him that sin left, wouldn't He be willing to do anything else for you? What could have cost Him more than His Son? So, when you're full of stress and fear and you ask Him for His help, it'll come. Without a second thought, the Lord will give you what you need. For Him, there's no pleasure in withholding hope from His children. Your cries for help will always be heard and will always be answered.

#110

Don't Do It Alone

Those who think they can do it on their own end up obsessed with measuring their own moral muscle but never get around to exercising it in real life.
ROMANS 8:6 MSG

Stop trying to do it on your own. You're incapable of making yourself good and acceptable. That mindset will only cause heartache. You may find success every now and again, but your power source is the Lord, and without Him, you'll eventually peter out. The human condition is limited, and allowing your sinful nature to control your mind will get you into trouble. Can you see that in your own life? A good way to avoid stress is to focus your mind on godly things—things you know are true and good. How do you do that? Ask the Spirit to control your thought-life; when He does, you'll find peace to replace the stress.

Stress from Doing the Right Thing

But even if you happen to suffer for doing what is right, you will have the joyful experience of the blessing of God. And don't be intimidated or terrified by those who would terrify you.

1 PETER 3:14 TPT

Keep your anxiety in perspective. Sometimes stress is inevitable and part of the suffering we'll face throughout our life. You might be stressed out because of backlash for standing up for what's right. You might feel rejected for going against the crowd and choosing God's way. You may even make a hard, moral choice that will put you in hot water at work. But that doesn't mean you're not blessed. The Lord hasn't abandoned you. Actually, you can be comforted by knowing God saw your hard decisions. He saw their judgmental responses. And He knows the stress and strife it caused to do the right thing. Stand tall, warrior woman. You are blessed.

He Will Always Take Care of You

When calamity comes, they will escape with their dignity. When famine invades the nations, they will be fed to their fill.

PSALM 37:19 VOICE

Let's settle this right here and now. The Lord will always take care of you. It's a promise! Your current situation may look bleak, but God is tracking with it. The future may seem unsettling, but He is already working things out for your good. Maybe you can't help but feel things are dark and desperate in some key relationships, but God will strengthen you and offer peace. He will be there to rescue you. He will save you. The Lord knows all the things that stress you and cause sleepless nights. And every time you cry out for Him, He hears you and promises to answer. Don't waste any more time with worry. Don't entertain anxiety. Instead, go right to the Lord. He's waiting!

#113

Don't Choke the Goodness

"The seed cast in the weeds is the person who hears the kingdom news, but weeds of worry and illusions about getting more and wanting everything under the sun strangle what was heard, and nothing comes of it."
MATTHEW 13:22 MSG

Don't be the kind of woman who hears the teachings of God but allows worry to choke the goodness away. While there are many opportunities to be concerned with this life, let the Word encourage you to trust. Let it challenge your old ways of responding to stressful situations. Spending time with the Lord is how your faith matures. And it's from those sacred spaces that fruit grows and becomes evident in your life. It's possible to keep stress at bay. With your focus on the Lord's promises, you can hold fast to the Truth rather than be tangled in the daily tension and trauma that finds you. God will give you confidence to stand against it.

#114

At All Times

He is ever present with me; at all times He goes before me. I will not live in fear or abandon my calling because He stands at my right hand.
PSALM 16:8 VOICE

With God, you can be fearless no matter what. Even if you feel all alone. Even when the deck seems stacked against you. Even when you feel judged. Even when your heart feels anxious. Even when life feels too big and your problems too messy. The truth is that God is always with you. He goes before you, clearing and highlighting the path, which is why you don't have to live in fear. You can stand strong in who God created you to be and do what He created you to do because He is with you at all times. Anxious thoughts have no room because the Lord fills every worrisome space with His love. Never forget that, friend. Let it be an anchor.

#115

The Pull of Anxiety

*And set your minds and keep them set
on what is above (the higher things),
not on the things that are on the earth.*
COLOSSIANS 3:2 AMPC

Anxiety grows when you obsess over all the things you can't change. It thrives when you stare at your hard circumstances and laughs as it delivers a big dose of hopelessness. It breeds when you turn your back on God's help and rewards you with sleepless nights. Anxiety partners with fear to make your situation almost unbearable so you become ineffective and paralyzed. This is why God's Word reminds you to set your mind on His promises, because it will keep you from constant worry. Focusing your time and attention on any earthly solution may offer a short-term fix, but it won't deliver to you the kind of freedom that God offers. It's only when you fix your eyes on God that you will overcome the pull of anxiety.

#116

He Will Wipe Away Every Tear

"He will wipe away every tear from their eyes and eliminate death entirely. No one will mourn or weep any longer. The pain of wounds will no longer exist, for the old order has ceased."

REVELATION 21:4 TPT

What pain from wounds are you dealing with right now? Are you reeling from a hard conversation with a friend? Are you hurting from rude comments from a spouse? Did someone at work step on your toes and take the credit for a job well done? Did your child break your heart with a bad decision? The truth is that all of these hurts cause anxiety for one reason or another. And as long as we're living in community with others, the opportunities for heartache will always be present. But there's hope when you take those stressors to God, because in the end He will wipe every tear from your eye. The hurts you're facing now will fade away, and peace will reign in your heart!

#117

What Are Your Motives?

"Examine your motives to make sure you're not showing off when you do your good deeds, only to be admired by others; otherwise, you will lose the reward of your heavenly Father."
MATTHEW 6:1 TPT

Stress comes from trying to impress others with how we live our life. Wanting someone to notice our good deeds causes anxiety because we're always performing for their approval. We become hypervigilant, which opens the door to worrying if they saw what we did. And if they did, were they awestruck? Did it captivate them? Friend, this is not a godly motive. Our goal shouldn't be to show off to others, hoping they will be fascinated and mesmerized. Instead, live in such a way that others want to know what makes your life different. Let your words and actions point to God in heaven. Let your life highlight Him and His goodness. There is no stress in that!

#118

Trying to Fit In

*Don't follow after the wicked ones or be
jealous of their wealth. Don't think for
a moment they're better off than you.*

PSALM 37:1 TPT

It can be stressful trying to fit into the "in crowd,"
especially when what makes them popular goes
against what you know is right. Maybe they drink
too much or flirt when their spouse isn't around.
Maybe they're always trying to cheat the system.
Maybe they spend money recklessly, and you can't
keep up. As much as you'd like to be part of their
group, your moral compass continues to sound the
alarm bell. There's anxiety as you walk the line
between living for Jesus and trying to fit into their
world. Ask the Lord for His perspective on the situation. Ask Him to show you what matters and what
doesn't. And ask God for the discernment so you
don't waste time pursuing the wrong things.

#119

What Are You Collecting?

Some people store up treasures in their homes here on earth. This is a shortsighted practice—don't undertake it. Moths and rust will eat up any treasure you may store here. Thieves may break into your homes and steal your precious trinkets.

MATTHEW 6:19 VOICE

It's okay to want your home to be inviting. Decorating the walls and shelves with items that make you happy is normal. Wanting visitors to get a homey feeling when they walk in your front door is caring. But it becomes an issue when you stress out about what others may think about the home you keep. When you're storing up treasures to impress others or fill an emptiness inside you, let it be a red flag. God is clear when He says to not store up goodies here on earth because they hold no eternal value. So, stressing out about creating the perfect home for you or others has no eternal reward attached. Heaven is your final destination, so choose to collect things with everlasting value.

#120

Rescued from the Tangles

*For He will rescue you from the snares
set by your enemies who entrap you
and from deadly plagues.*
PSALM 91:3 VOICE

Sometimes we just need to be rescued from the mess in which we're entangled. While our choices can land us in peril, they're not always conscious decisions. We're not always out looking for trouble, right? Regardless, it's stressful to be stuck in our situation. Not being able to find freedom is disheartening at best; and when we are trapped, it's the perfect time to cry out to God for help. He promises to save us when we can't save ourselves. He guarantees to be ready and willing to jump feet first into our mess to free us. And honestly, when you humbly ask the Lord to take control of the anxiety-ridden situations you're wedged in, He will.

#121

Compelled to Protect

*Like a bird protecting its young, God will cover
you with His feathers, will protect you under His
great wings; His faithfulness will form a shield
around you, a rock-solid wall to protect you.*
PSALM 91:4 VOICE

Chances are you understand the mentality of protecting your own, especially if you're a mother—be it by birth, adoption, or as a spiritual mentor. There's something that rises up in you when someone you care about is hurting. In those moments, your heart races as the blood pumps through your veins. Your protective instinct kicks in, and you're ready for action. The adrenaline empowers you to act. Now think about how much more capable God is to care for and protect us with His perfect love. When He sees you weighed down by worry or fear, His first response is to cover you under His wing. He forms a shield around you. He becomes like a rock wall to protect you from what is causing stress and strife. What a beautiful visual of God's love and compassion.

#122

The Stressful Fall of Others

A thousand may fall on your left, ten thousand may die on your right, but these horrors won't come near you. Only your eyes will witness the punishment that awaits the evil, but you will not suffer because of it.
PSALM 91:7–8 VOICE

When you are walking with the Lord, don't let the fall of those around you stress you out as you worry if you're next. It's scary to see people suffer the natural consequences of their actions. It's destabilizing when someone you held in high regard has sin exposed. In those times, ask the Lord for protection for your heart as you navigate through the grief. Ask Him to build your courage and confidence in Him so you don't fall into the pit of anxiousness. Ask for wisdom to discern your next steps carefully, following His leading. Share with God every emotion coursing through your veins as you process what your eyes are seeing. And if there is anything you need to confess, let it be a worrisome weight lifted off your shoulders.

Your Place of Residence

Because you've made the LORD my refuge, the Most High, your place of residence—no evil will happen to you; no disease will come close to your tent.
PSALM 91:9–10 CEB

When you realize the expectations you had in your relationship were unrealistic, talk to the Lord. When you worked hard for something that didn't come to pass, leaving you heartbroken, pray about it. When the test results reveal a condition that wasn't even a concern at the time, share your fear with God. Every time life throws you a curve ball, make Him your place of residence. Run for His covering. Let the Lord be your refuge and protection. God is the only safe place where you can be fully seen and fully known. He is trustworthy. He is faithful. And rather than try to fix things yourself or rely on worldly solutions, lean into the love of the One who created you.

When Doubt Makes You Sink

*Instantly Jesus reached out His hand
and caught and held him, saying to him,
O you of little faith, why did you doubt?*
MATTHEW 14:31 AMPC

Doubting is part of the human condition. When you are full of worry, it's because you doubt things will work out to your advantage. Being anxious indicates you're not certain of the actions being taken. The truth is that nothing in this world is guaranteed. Too often, rather than go right to God with our stress, we sit in the heartache and doubt. Peter was fine to get out on the water and walk toward Jesus, but the waves made him question his safety, and He began to sink. Notice, though, that the Lord reached out and saved Peter from going under. He wasn't punished for doubting. Jesus caught and held him. Trust that He will do the same for you.

In Plain Sight

*Lord, my longings are sitting in plain sight,
my groans an old story to you. My heart's
about to break; I'm a burned-out case.*
PSALM 38:9–10 MSG

Rarely do we like feeling exposed. We're not usually big fans of having our moments of weakness hanging out there for all to see. Being vulnerable is tricky for a heart that's been trampled on and beaten up in the past. Most of the time, we try to keep our anxiety tucked away. We try to hide it so we look like we have it all together. We don't want others to know that deep down we're terrified and freaked out. But God wants you to find relief that your tangled heart is in plain sight to Him. He is a safe place to be messy. You can let every fear and worry show. Trust that He will always offer help when you're feeling overwhelmed by life.

#126

The Reason to Stay Rooted

God says, "Because you are devoted
to me, I'll rescue you. I'll protect you
because you know my name."
PSALM 91:14 CEB

If there was ever a compelling reason to stay rooted in and connected to the Lord, today's verse reveals it. God makes a clear connection between your desire for a relationship with Him and His response to your needs. The Lord honors those who show devotion—like spending time in the Bible, choosing to follow His ways, and making time to pray—by rescuing them from stress and strife. When anxiety spikes and it's God's name on your lips, it makes a difference to Him. Leaning into the Lord because you trust His character and promises doesn't go unnoticed. And when He is the One you cry out to in fearful moments, He will always strengthen you with courage and confidence.

Overwhelmed, Swamped, Submerged

*I'm overwhelmed, swamped, and submerged
beneath the heavy burden of my guilt.
It clings to me and won't let me go.*
PSALM 38:4 TPT

Few things bring on anxiety like guilt. We worry we'll be found out, causing others to be disappointed in our choices. We worry the lies we told will catch up to us and leave us humiliated. We stress about what our actions have done to those we love, scared they will be scarred forever. Guilt has a special way of making us feel overwhelmed, swamped, and submerged. Here is good news for your weary heart. The Lord already knows your guilt. He understands your motives better than you do. He sees your fears, and that makes Him the best One to run to for help. Without condemnation, the Lord will help you find relief so you can live in the freedom Jesus died for.

#128

Liquid Words

Lord, you know all my desires and
deepest longings. My tears are liquid
words and you can read them all.
PSALM 38:9 TPT

Every stress-filled tear that rolls down your cheek is seen by God. Not one falls without Him noticing. Even more, the Lord knows what worry that tear represents. He fully understands what made it fall in the first place. The Bible says your tears are liquid words and God reads them all. When your marriage is a mess, He knows. When you're scared for the future, He sees. When your child's mental health is shaky, the Lord recognizes the stress. Friend, let the truth that He knows every worry and fear bring peace to your weary soul. You're fully known by the One who will save and restore. He'll bring peace and comfort. And He never misses a liquid word.

#129

He Won't Desert or Disown You

*So don't forsake me now, Lord! Don't leave me
in this condition. God, hurry to help me, run to
my rescue! For you're my Savior and my only hope!*
Psalm 38:21–22 TPT

Settle in your heart today this powerful truth: God
will never abandon you. He won't ever desert you.
He won't leave or disown you. The Lord won't reject you no matter what you do. He will never quit
on you. God won't renounce you or give you up.
And friend, the Lord won't ever turn His back to
you. When your anxious thoughts lead you down
the trail that says you aren't lovable or important,
turn around. When old memories of rejection or
abandonment convince you that's how God feels
about you, rebuke it. Run right to God and share
your anxious heart. Then watch how He empowers
you with confidence in His unshakable love once
again.

#130

The Gravity of Rejection

*My heart beats wildly, my strength is sapped,
and the light of my eyes is going out. My friends
stay far away from me, avoiding me like the plague.
Even my family wants nothing to do with me.*

PSALM 38:10–11 TPT

When we experience rejection from friends and family, it messes us up. It taps into feelings of worthlessness. These people are supposed to be there through thick and thin. They're who we lean on in hard times. And when we're left all alone, anxiety skyrockets as our greatest fears come to light. How do we make sense of these situations? How can we trust again? Why risk putting ourselves out there one more time? This is when we run to God and ask Him to calm our fears. We ask Him to comfort our broken heart. We let Him restore our sense of value. In these moments, let the Lord be your safe place. He won't ever let you down.

#131

Not Rooted in Worry

"But be on your guard. Don't let the sharp edge of your expectation get dulled by parties and drinking and shopping."
LUKE 21:34 MSG

God asks you to be ready for His Son's return. He wants you to be sharp and crisp, because this amazing moment can come at any time. Although God doesn't want you to live stressed out about it, He hopes for intentionality. Sometimes those kinds of anxious thoughts control us. We obsess over them, trying to make sure everything is in order. We worry we've missed something or aren't doing the right things. This isn't how God wants us to be. When He asks you to be on guard, He's asking you to live with passion and purpose, and these requests aren't rooted in worry. They are rooted in faith. And that's exactly where the Lord is hoping you'll stay.

#132

Be Gentle with Others

*Make a clean break with all cutting, backbiting,
profane talk. Be gentle with one another, sensitive.
Forgive one another as quickly and thoroughly
as God in Christ forgave you.*
EPHESIANS 4:31–32 MSG

Be gentle with others. When those we care about
are struggling, we often tell them to push through.
Our advice is to buck up and make it happen. We
try to encourage by telling them to just put on their
big girl pants and get 'er done. While our motives
may be good, those kinds of words aren't gentle.
They come across as harsh and increase rather
than lower stress levels. In their state of worry, our
loved ones don't receive our words as we intended
them, and their feelings are hurt. It's so important
to love others well. We need to choose our words
carefully, treat others with respect, and forgive
quickly. When we do, we won't be the cause of any
stress and strife in their life.

#133

The Reason We Wait

*Lord, the only thing I can do is wait and put
my hope in you. I wait for your help, my God.*
PSALM 38:15 TPT

Hold on, dear one. When stress is overwhelming, hold on. When anxiety steals your sleep, keep talking to God. When you cannot stop worrying about horrible outcomes and endings, continue praying. When your concerns feel too heavy to carry, don't give up hope. Sometimes we have to wait on the Lord to remove the weariness of the road we're walking. It's not because He doesn't hear us. It's not because He is punishing us or doesn't have time. But there are important things we learn along the way—tools we need in our toolbelt. So, find the resolve to wait for God's help, knowing it will arrive at the perfect moment. And, yes, it will always come.

#134

The Call to Live in Peace

Don't hit back; discover beauty in everyone.
If you've got it in you, get along with everybody.
Don't insist on getting even; that's not for you to do.
"I'll do the judging," says God. "I'll take care of it."
ROMANS 12:18–19 MSG

God wants you to be a peacemaker. His hope is for every one of us to do what needs to be done to get along. Sometimes that means we choose not to be offended. It means we don't sit in judgment of those around us. Other times, it means we have hard conversations to clear the air and restore harmony to our relationships. Maybe the Lord wants us to live in peace so we aren't weighed down by worry. Maybe God's hope is that His children grab the freedom His Son died for, knowing that anxiety would make it impossible. Regardless of the *why*, trust that God wants you to live in peace for good reasons. . . and make it a priority in your life.

#135

The Battle with Sleeplessness

Now, because of you, Lord, I will lie down in peace and sleep comes at once, for no matter what happens, I will live unafraid!
PSALM 4:8 TPT

Have you ever struggled to sleep because of anxiety? No doubt, sweet slumber is most often a casualty of a worried heart. It's usually in the quiet of night that our minds won't stop long enough to let us rest. They take us down pathways of hopelessness and angst as we see no good outcome of the situation we're struggling with. God knew this would be something to plague us. He knew the challenges that fear and worry would bring. And because of them, the Lord promised us the power of His presence. So, the next time you're wrestling with anxiousness at night, ask Him to bring comfort. Ask Him to calm your fears. And friend, choose to give it to God and then go to sleep.

#136

Stress-Buster Decisions

*Walk away from the evil things in the world—
just leave them behind, and do what is right,
and always seek peace and pursue it.*

1 PETER 3:11 VOICE

When we're not doing what we know is the right thing, it's stressful. Maybe not at first, but once our moral compass is righted and we understand the consequences that may follow our choices, anxiety eventually sets in. Choosing to entertain sinful ways sets us up for heartbreak. It opens the door to fear and sorrow. Today's verse calls us higher. It's a challenge to live with intentionality. And when we make the choice to walk away from ungodly living, we also walk away from the stress that comes with it. God's Word makes it clear that He blesses our obedience. He honors our righteousness. Taking a stand and making sure our life is full of passion and purpose are stress-buster decisions with far-reaching blessings.

#137

The Choice Is Yours

No one can serve two masters. If you try, you will wind up loving the first master and hating the second, or vice versa. People try to serve both God and money— but you can't. You must choose one or the other.
MATTHEW 6:24 VOICE

It's easy to get pulled in two different directions. The struggle is real, amen? You may have every good intention to focus your time, talent, and treasure on godly things, like following God's commands; being generous, loving, and forgiving; and spending time in the Word. But the world's pull is often so strong. Anxiety comes from teetering on the ledge between the two. You know the choices you're making may not be the right ones, but the evidence is compelling. The Lord doesn't mince words when He says you have to choose one or the other. The choice is yours to make. And the truth is that following God may not always be stress-free, but it will bring blessings. Even more, God will give you all you need to make it possible.

#138

Flawless

*Our faith in Jesus transfers God's righteousness
to us and he now declares us flawless in his eyes.
This means we can now enjoy true and lasting
peace with God, all because of what our Lord
Jesus, the Anointed One, has done for us.*

ROMANS 5:1 TPT

When you start to feel anxious about your relationship with God, wondering if you've pushed Him
too far this time, take a deep breath. You're not
capable of making the Lord walk away from you.
Regardless of the bad choices you've made, you've
been made right with God because of your faith. He
doesn't have expectations that you will be flawless
on your own. Instead, the Lord completely understands your need for a savior. He knew sin would
enter the world and separate you from Him. So,
God sent His Son, Jesus, to bridge the gap. His death
is what makes peace possible. It's why you don't
have to stress about being good enough for God. It's
why you are now flawless in His eyes.

#139

Stress Relief from the Word

The people who love your Instruction enjoy peace—
and lots of it. There's no stumbling for them!
PSALM 119:165 CEB

One of the best ways to lower your stress level is to dig into the Word of God. In its pages, you will find deep encouragement to stand strong. You'll find testimonies of everyday people who battled the same kinds of anxiety as you. You'll learn how they became overcomers, and you will be challenged to put your full faith in the Lord. The Word will call you higher and ask you to give up control. It will tell you how to find lasting peace and comfort. The Bible will unpack the secrets to living and loving well. So, the next time panic sets in and you are battling fear and worry, grab the Word of God, and saturate yourself in its truths. God will meet you there.

#140

Not a God of Confusion

When we worship the right way,
God doesn't stir us up into confusion;
he brings us into harmony.
1 CORINTHIANS 14:33 MSG

God is not a God of confusion. He doesn't bring mayhem and chaos into the circumstances you're struggling with. He isn't the reason your emotions are stirred up. The cause of your stress and strife has nothing to do with the Lord. What a gift to have scripture point that out, because it settles in your heart and mind that God is a safe place. When you're weary from the health battle, worried about the fight with your spouse, or concerned for the upcoming test, know that God will always help and not hinder. And if you ask, He will bring a powerful peace into your situation that nothing or no one else can.

#141

Living in Peace

The seed that flowers into righteousness
will always be planted in peace by
those who embrace peace.
JAMES 3:18 VOICE

Can you imagine what it would feel like to live in peace? No more stress reigning in your relationships. No more worry about your children's choices weighing you down. No more fear of what your future may look like. No more consuming concern about the bills coming your way. When you choose to live in peaceful ways, your heart will find rest. Your emotions won't be on a crazy roller-coaster ride. Drama won't be a go-to response. And you won't sit in a victim-mentality tailspin. But it takes an intentional choice every day to embrace the kind of peace the Lord offers. When you ask Him for help to live in peaceful ways, you will be blessed by it.

#142

Walk As the Wise

So be careful how you live; be mindful of your steps.
Don't run around like idiots as the rest of the
world does. Instead, walk as the wise!

EPHESIANS 5:15 VOICE

When you walk as the wise, it brings a calmness into your circumstances. Your heart is at rest, and your mind isn't racing, full of horrible outcomes and endings. The reason is because you've put in the time and effort with the Lord to help you make choices that reflect your faith. They glorify God. That decision to choose wisely and be mindful of how you live results in an unexplainable sense of peace. And it's His peace that has the power to calm anxiety and stress like nothing else. The world holds no answers for you, friend. It offers only shortcuts and short-term options that lead nowhere. Don't look to it for help. Instead, let God's wisdom flow through you and usher in stress-free living.

A Willingness to Listen and Learn

*Listen well to wise counsel and be willing
to learn from correction so that by the end of
your life you'll be known for your wisdom.*
PROVERBS 19:20 TPT

God often speaks through those who love us. He uses those relationships that matter the most to encourage us along the way. We should always meditate on their words and ask for God's confirmation before we act, because community has an amazing way to bless us with wise counsel. So, when you're worried about a big decision, talk to those you trust. When you feel stressed about which next step is the right one, talk it through with your mentors. When you are seeing red flags in a relationship that scares you, unpack it with someone who will be honest with you. And always be willing to listen and learn, because doing so trains you to be smarter and wiser. Even more, that wisdom will help curb the ups and downs of anxiety so you can live in peace.

#144

A Teachable Heart

A fool is in love with his own opinion,
but wisdom means being teachable.
PROVERBS 12:15 TPT

How much anxiety could be skipped if we decided to be more teachable? Too often, we dig in our heels to do things our way and end up stressed out. Thinking our way is the best way is prideful and dangerous. While we are smart women with sound life experience, we don't have all the answers to life's questions. So think about it, friend. What keeps you from taking advice from those who can offer hard-won wisdom? Why don't you seek counsel from those you trust? Stress can be avoided in certain situations by humbly asking for guidance. And choosing to have a teachable heart will help you avoid unwanted worry and fear. Asking for help is always a good idea.

#145

When You Feel Bullied

Take my side, God—I'm getting kicked around,
stomped on every day. Not a day goes by but somebody
beats me up; they make it their duty to beat me up.
Psalm 56:1–2 msg

When you feel bullied by someone, it creates deep trenches of stress in your heart. It makes you question your goodness. You wonder if all the horrible things they say about you are true. You struggle with self-worth and a personal sense of safety. And these feelings usher you right into anxiety. If you're struggling with this right now, please tell someone. There is no place for this in your life. When you are being buried under layers of anxiety, you become ineffective in every area of your life. This kind of stress affects every relationship. It clouds every decision. And it takes a toll on your mental health. Ask God to show you the next step. . .and then take it.

#146

How to Be Fearless

When I get really afraid I come to you in trust.
I'm proud to praise God; fearless now, I trust
in God. What can mere mortals do?
PSALM 56:3–4 MSG

Fear never fights fair and often shows up unexpectedly. It shakes your confidence and makes you doubt people and plans. Being afraid is a horrible feeling. In those fearful moments, what do you do? To whom do you turn? Where do you look for help? The psalmist in today's verse shows confidence by going right to God with trust and praise. He knows the Lord will be faithful to bring a sense of peace to override any fear. And once the comfort comes, the courage does too. His praise spills out as his perspective realigns. Can you see the bold confidence? Let God be your first stop when you start to feel afraid. Let Him make you fearless and brave!

#147

Energized by God

*I'm energized every time I enter your heavenly
sanctuary to seek more of your power
and drink in more of your glory.*
PSALM 63:2 TPT

God gives us strength and power to stand up to anxious thoughts. He will energize us to stand strong when our marriage is rocky. He'll give us courage to stand up for what we believe when faced with a choice. God will deliver confidence to dispel the joy-draining lies that whisper in our ear and will replace them with His powerful truth. And when asked, the Lord will bring freedom from stress and anxiety. As women living in a crazy world, worry will be ever-present. But you get to choose what to do with it. You choose how it affects you. You decide if it's a constant companion. Ask the Lord to energize you with hope and faith, and live free!

#148

All the Way in Heaven

[If] My people (who are known by My name) humbly pray, follow My commandments, and abandon any actions or thoughts that might lead to further sinning, then I shall hear their prayers from My house in heaven, I shall forgive their sins, and I shall save their land from the disasters.

2 CHRONICLES 7:14 VOICE

The Lord hears you every time you call out in worry. When your anxious thoughts overwhelm you, God sees the tears that fall. When you beg Him for relief from stress, He always notices. What a gift to know that God's ear is always listening for your voice! He is always waiting to hear from you. And even more, there is nothing that can steal His attention away from your needs. All the way from heaven, God watches over you with great interest and intention. Oh, how He loves you! So be willing to be vulnerable with the Lord. Be honest about the issues causing concern. And humbly pray that God will prompt you to reach out to Him for help when life feels too overwhelming.

#149

Bite-Size Faith

The Lord is for me—I won't be afraid. What can anyone do to me? The Lord is for me—as my helper. I look in victory on those who hate me.
PSALM 118:6–7 CEB

If God is for you then who can be against you? Those are powerful words that carry great weight because they're essentially saying you are in a saving relationship with the Lord; therefore, you shouldn't stress over anything. They are saying you shouldn't have any fear for the tangling situations before you. The worrisome threats from others are null and void. And because God promises to help any time you need Him, peace should reign in your heart as you trust He will handle it all. Honestly, this isn't easy to walk out. We've all had our hearts broken, so sometimes this requires big faith. Why not take one step at a time, trusting the Lord in small, bite-size chunks?

#150

No Weapon Formed Against You Wins

But no instrument forged against you will be allowed to hurt you, and no voice raised to condemn you will successfully prosecute you. It's that simple; this is how it will be for the servants of the Eternal; I will vindicate them.

ISAIAH 54:17 VOICE

Does it feel like the walls are caving in? Maybe your bloodwork showed an area of concern or the treatment isn't working. Maybe your company is downsizing, and you were let go. Maybe you can't seem to process through the grief and feel stuck in it. Maybe you feel alone after the divorce and are worried this is your new normal. Maybe your reputation is being attacked by others. Take heart! You may be feeling the stress deep in your bones, but the Lord promises that no weapon formed against you shall prosper. He promises no voice meant to condemn you will succeed. And your Father promises to defend you until the end. Deep breath, friend. God has you covered.

#151

Return to the Lord

Return to the LORD your God, for he is merciful and compassionate, very patient, full of faithful love, and ready to forgive.
JOEL 2:13 CEB

In your stress and strife, have you walked away from God? Do you criticize Him for all the things that went wrong? In your mind, is He the reason you're stuck in your situation? Friend, anxiety is so full of confusion. It's not unimaginable to begin blaming God for where you are right now. But the truth is that He wouldn't do anything to hurt you, and the Bible backs that up throughout its pages. Even more, your power to overcome anxiety rests in Him. So, in faith, why not choose to believe the Lord. Talk to Him right now. Ask for His help, because God is merciful and compassionate, very patient, full of love for you, and ready to aid you.

#152

Eyes on Jesus

When they finally opened their eyes and looked around, they saw no one else there but Jesus.
MATTHEW 17:8 TPT

Think back to a time when anxiety was so over-whelming you just squeezed your eyes tightly shut. Maybe you were at the end of your rope. Maybe you were fighting back tears. Maybe you were ready to give up. Regardless, go back to that place. Now imagine that you finally open your eyes and all you see is Jesus. The fear is gone. The stress has left. The worry melts away. And the Savior is all you can see. Friend, this is possible for you every day. Whenever anxiety feels too heavy, keep your focus on Jesus. Tell Him you trust Him. Tell the Lord you have faith in Him. And whenever your anxious thoughts try to get your attention, close your eyes and open them again on Jesus.

#153

Surrounded No More

*No longer will I fear my tens of thousands
of enemies who have surrounded me!*
PSALM 3:6 VOICE

We've all felt the stress that comes from being attacked on every side. There are times we feel it on every front, amen? Like when our finances are too tight or we're in a rough patch in our marriage. Or when our kids are struggling in school and we're exhausted from overtime at work. Or maybe when aging parents are too demanding while we're still grieving loss. These seasons can often feel like tens of thousands of enemies surrounding our sense of peace every day. Decide right now that when this kind of stress invades our life again, we will call on the name of Jesus. He is with us and for us. And when we invite Him into the mess, He will remove the fear, and we will find harmony again!

#154

Bringing Your Soul Back to Fullness

When your soul is famished and withering,
He fills you with good and beautiful things,
satisfying you as long as you live. He makes
you strong like an eagle, restoring your youth.

PSALM 103:5 VOICE

We may look to worldly things to satisfy our longings. We may try earthly remedies to fill our emptiness or relieve our stress. We may even put all our hope in processes or people, assuming the right combination will make us feel better about our situation. But these are short-lived answers that do nothing to bring our famished and withered soul back to fullness. Trust the Lord to meet those needs. Trust that He will saturate you with His love, which will renew your strength. Nothing can replicate the healing and restorative power of God. With His help, the stress and anxiety will lose their hold on you. Peace will replace the worry. So, let Him be the One to satisfy!

#155

Let His Love Overwhelm You

Lord, you're so kind and tenderhearted to those who don't deserve it and so patient with people who fail you! Your love is like a flooding river overflowing its banks with kindness. You don't look at us only to find our faults, just so that you can hold a grudge against us.

PSALM 103:8–9 TPT

So often in our stress and strife, we turn our backs on the Lord. We may not blame Him for our circumstances, but we go into fix-it mode alone. We circle our own wagons, trying to manipulate or control the situation. We develop tunnel vision and are able to see only the anxiousness in front of us. We rely on ourselves above all else. It must grieve the heart of God to watch you suffer this way, friend. You were never meant to carry it alone. His constant invitation is to lay your worries and fears at His feet in exchange for His kindness and tenderheartedness. Open your heart to His extraordinary compassion and promise to save you. Let His love overwhelm you.

He Will Remove It

Farther than from a sunrise to a sunset—
that's how far you've removed our guilt from us.
PSALM 103:12 TPT

Guilt and stress go hand in hand. Are you feeling guilty right now? Maybe you yelled at the kids or betrayed a friend's confidence. Maybe you dismissed your husband's request for help or ignored the budget. Maybe you lied at work or didn't show up to volunteer. Wherever the guilt came from, chances are you're struggling with anxious thoughts surrounding it. The Lord wants to take it away because He knows it messes with your sense of peace. He understands it buries you with stress as you replay the offense over and over again. And when you confess and ask, God will completely remove it. There may be some natural consequences to weather, but your heart will be at peace and your anxiety will be at zero.

#157

He Knows It All

You know all about us, inside and out.
You are mindful that we're made from dust.
PSALM 103:14 TPT

Sometimes it's hard to find the words to describe all the ways our emotions are stirred up. Anxiety clouds clarity. And when we feel overwhelmed by a situation, so often the words never come. We struggle to share because we don't know how to unpack the complexity of our emotions to others. So we stress out in silence, trapped. The good news is that God already knows what's inside your heart and mind. Even more, He absolutely understands every bit of it—even the parts that feel confusing to you. God recognizes what triggered the anxiety. He knows the origin of the worry. And the Lord has already gone before you to straighten the crooked path you're walking. So talk to God about it.

#158

But God Is Bigger

Bless God, all creatures, wherever you are—
everything and everyone made by God.
PSALM 103:22 MSG

When you start to feel like your anxiety is too big, remember God is bigger. When the stress from your marriage, the fear of your future, or the worry over your child's school year looks more like a mountain than a molehill, remember God is above everything. His kingdom rules over all. He has dominion over everything that happens, so don't allow your anxious heart to overinflate itself. Nothing has permission to gain superiority over the Lord, and that is wonderful news! It means that when stress creeps in, you can give it to God and watch Him crush it. Let nothing in your life take the high and mighty place of God, especially nothing that threatens your peace and joy!

#159

Your Weakness Isn't a Deficit

But he answered me, "My grace is always more than enough for you, and my power finds its full expression through your weakness." So I will celebrate my weaknesses, for when I'm weak I sense more deeply the mighty power of Christ living in me.

2 CORINTHIANS 12:9 TPT

Have you ever considered that your freak-out moments are actually moments where God can shine most brightly? He says His grace is enough, and we learn in His Word that our weakness isn't a deficit. Instead, this is when God's power can break through. Ask God to let it be true for you. Remember, your struggle is an opportunity to shine Jesus to others, so ask the Lord to shine bright into your weak areas for your benefit and for others to see. Invite His power to live in you and through you!

#160

Don't Let Stress Hinder Doing Good

So watch your step. Use your head. Make the most of every chance you get. These are desperate times!

EPHESIANS 5:16 MSG

If God wants you to use every opportunity that comes your way to do good in the world, anxiety will most certainly keep you from it. It's hard to be kind to others when our stress level is off the charts. We can't be effective in ministry if we're clutching unforgiveness, agitated at someone for hurting our feelings. Our relationships will suffer when we aren't full of love and compassion, when we're concerned more with being right than getting along. It's so important that we are careful with how we live in community. It's a gift from the Lord. And when we allow fretting and fussing to be our guide, it will cause great pain all the way around.

It's Going to Be All Right

"I called out your name, O GOD, called from
the bottom of the pit. You listened when I
called out, 'Don't shut your ears! Get me out
of here! Save me!' You came close when I
called out. You said, 'It's going to be all right.' "
LAMENTATIONS 3:55–57 MSG

It may seem overwhelming, but it will work out. Things may feel way too big at the moment, but you will survive. You may want to crawl into bed and wave the white flag, but you're stronger than you think. The news may have knocked you to your knees, but it won't overtake you. Your heart may be beating out of your chest, but the Lord is near. These are the times we cry out to God for help. From the bottom of the pit, we look up for His help. This is when we drop to our knees and beg God to show up big-time and fill us with His peace. And this is when He pulls us close and says, "It's going to be all right."

#162

How to Be Brave

*Then Jesus said, "Be brave and
don't be afraid. I am here."*
MATTHEW 14:27 TPT

Sometimes being brave is a tall order because
there's not one bone in our body that feels that way.
The opposite of bravery is anxiety, and when that's
reigning in our hearts and minds, it's impossible to
find the courage to move forward in a meaningful
way. We're more frantic than confident, amen? But
God's presence has a way of draining the stress so
we can stand strong against any opposition. In those
moments where you feel fear closing in on you, ask
the Lord to be near. Ask Him to calm your anxious
heart. Ask for the peace of Jesus to fall on you right
then and there so you can catch your breath and
gather your thoughts. . .and be brave.

#163

He'll Bring Victory

The Lord your God is in your midst—a warrior bringing victory. He will create calm with his love; he will rejoice over you with singing.
ZEPHANIAH 3:17 CEB

When you trust God with the things creating anxiety, you experience victory from them. Talk to Him every time those fears pop up. Tell Him the minute your heart starts pounding and your face starts sweating. Whenever your chest tightens from the stress, let the Lord be your first responder. There's power in the name of Jesus, and He is mighty to save! He promises to bring calmness because His love for you is so great. God will sing over you, rejoicing for how extraordinary He made you. With Him by your side, there's nothing too big to handle or too difficult to overcome. The Lord is a warrior, and together you will find victory for the anxiety that threatens your peace.

#164

Be Secure in Your Faith

*They will not live in fear or dread
of what may come, for their hearts
are firm, ever secure in their faith.*
PSALM 112:7 TPT

If your faith isn't secure in the Lord, fear may always be an issue. It is easy to be afraid in this world because it's full of evil. There are countless reasons for anxiety to overtake us. We worry for our family and friends because we know what's out there, and we know we can't protect them at every turn. But don't live in hopelessness! Scripture clearly says when your heart is firm in your relationship with the Lord and your faith is anchored in Him, you won't succumb to fear. You won't live with a sense of dread. Remember, the key is trusting God over everything else. That choice will allow you to raise your head and see hope!

#165

It's Okay to Expect

*Their hearts are confident, and they
are fearless, for they expect to see
their enemies defeated.*
PSALM 112:8 VOICE

Would your anxiety level be manageable if you expected God to show up in stressful situations? When the weight of worry feels too heavy, would knowing that God is working things out on your behalf help? If you answered yes to either question, take heart! The Lord says this kind of confidence holds great power because it's drenched in faith. It's choosing to trust God's Word. It's closing the door to fear and focusing on truth. Friend, it's right to assume the Lord will battle whatever causes stress in your life. You can confidently expect Him to usher in peace instead. And you can know He will always fight for you.

It's Time to Take Charge

David continued to address Solomon: "Take charge! Take heart! Don't be anxious or get discouraged. GOD, my God, is with you in this; he won't walk off and leave you in the lurch. He's at your side until every last detail is completed for conducting the worship of GOD."
1 CHRONICLES 28:20 MSG

Don't let anxiety keep you from doing the next right thing. With God's help, you can move forward while keeping your eyes focused on Him rather than on what's stirring you up. You must, friend. There are people depending on you right now. You bring talents and giftings unmatched by others. And when you cower under stress, you're rendered ineffective. Just as David said to Solomon, this is your time to take charge! Remember, God isn't asking you to handle the anxiety on your own. He won't leave you to figure it out alone. Instead, He is with you until every detail is done. And when you ask, He will encourage your heart all along the way. You can do this!

Don't Focus on the Enemy

When you go forth to battle against your enemies and see horses and chariots and an army greater than your own, do not be afraid of them, for the Lord your God, Who brought you out of the land of Egypt, is with you.

DEUTERONOMY 20:1 AMPC

Today's verse is a beautiful reminder to keep your eyes on God. Why is the Lord asking this of you? Because your enemies often look stronger and bigger. They look more ferocious. They look more coordinated with better strategy and skill. And when you focus on them, your heart becomes anxious. You automatically feel defeated because it looks like you're outnumbered or outsmarted. And while they may look formidable enough to strike fear in your spirit, never forget that God is bigger! No one is above Him. No one is stronger. And when you think back to all the times He saved you, healed you, and provided for you, your faith is reignited. Let that be why your heart is calm and your faith is strong.

#168

A Circle of Protection

*God's angel sets up a circle of
protection around us while we pray.*
PSALM 34:7 MSG

What a beautiful and powerful image of how God protects those He loves. Don't miss it. As we cry out to the Lord and ask for deliverance from our fears, we are protected on every side. When we go to God with our insecurities, we're encircled in His safety. Every time we open up to Him about those things causing anxiety, there is a divine defensive surrounding us. Why is this so significant? Because it removes any barrier to us fully pouring out our hearts to Him. We don't have to worry that we're exposed or vulnerable in that moment. Instead, we can pray with confidence, knowing we can focus solely on that time in prayer. It's sacred space that's safeguarded.

I Won't Be Shaken

When evil ones come to destroy me, they will be the ones who turn back. My heart will not be afraid even if an army rises to attack. I know that you are there for me, so I will not be shaken.

PSALM 27:2–3 TPT

When you feel attacked or oppressed by someone, it's stressful. Few things cause anxiety more than feeling like everyone is against you. Loneliness is a horrible reality that we all face from time to time. But notice in today's verse that the writer has a bold confidence in God's presence to keep him safe. He knows he's not alone! And it's that truth that keeps him steady. It's why he isn't freaking out even when his eyes see chaos and confusion. He knows the Lord is always with him and always for him. So, when worry begins to take up space in your heart, speak this out loud: *I know God is here for me so I will not be shaken.* He's got you.

#170

Asking for Clarity

*Now teach me all about your ways and tell me
what to do. Make it clear for me to understand,
for I am surrounded by waiting enemies.*
PSALM 27:11 TPT

Let God be the One to help you navigate the anxious feelings you're having. Rather than hide from stressors, go right to God, and ask Him what to do. Don't depend on your friends or family to have the answers; He sees the situation in its entirety. They may want the best for you, but the Lord knows the right path to follow. And when your mind feels chaotic from worry and fear, ask Him to provide you with clarity. Let God help you make sense of the stress-filled situation you're facing in your marriage. Let Him gently straighten the crooked path you're walking at work. Be quick to run toward the Lord for wisdom and discernment as you parent. Nothing can be stacked against you when God is involved.

#171

One More Time

Yet I totally trust you to rescue me one more time,
so that I can see once again how good you are
while I'm still alive! Here's what I've learned
through it all: Don't give up; don't be impatient;
be entwined as one with the Lord. Be brave and
courageous, and never lose hope. Yes, keep on
waiting—for he will never disappoint you!
PSALM 27:13–14 TPT

When you find yourself trapped in anxiety, God will rescue you every time. In those moments of apprehension, hold on to the truth that the Lord is mighty to save one more time. There is no reason to give up. Don't throw in the towel. Don't cower in fear and frustration. God is working! He may not pull you from stress on demand, but He will in His perfect timing. And when you activate your faith, you will always find courage to hold on when things feel overwhelming. He isn't a God who disappoints! He is a God who delivers over and over and over again!

Let Him Know How You Feel

*Listen to them bragging among themselves,
big in their own eyes, all because of the crimes
they've committed against your people! See
how they're crushing those who love you, God,
cruelly oppressing those who belong to you.*

PSALM 94:4–5 TPT

When you talk to God about what others are doing to cause stress and strife, it's not gossiping. You can dish with the Divine in great detail, freely sharing your frustrations and fears. As a matter of fact, God invites you to bare your soul to Him and holds none of it against you. Be honest about how that person is causing anxiety. Be real with how their actions have made you feel. Be vulnerable with how you unpack your thoughts. You can say what you think and feel without condemnation. Let the Lord be your safe place to purge everything in your heart— the good, the bad, the ugly. You will never turn Him off with your transparency.

#173

He Never Changes

Jesus the Anointed One is always the same:
yesterday, today, and forever.
HEBREWS 13:8 VOICE

Does change stress you out? For so many of us, change has the power to wreck us, especially when it's unexpected. We get comfortable in our bubble of predictability where we know what comes next. It's safe. It's secure. And it lets us maintain control. When life takes a surprising left turn, it sets into motion layer upon layer of anxiety. We panic. Rather than embrace the change, we freak out. Here's some good news: God is the same today as He was yesterday and will be the same tomorrow. You can always count on stability with Him. His character never changes. So, when a curve ball comes out of nowhere, cling to the One who promises to steady your heart.

#174

There Is a Season

*For everything that happens in life—
there is a season, a right time for
everything under heaven.*
ECCLESIASTES 3:1 VOICE

It's important to remember that when you're in a difficult time in life where the deck seems to be stacked against you, it's just a season. It will pass. On the flip side, remember that when you feel on top of the world and life is treating you right, that's a season too. Life ebbs and flows by design. Everything can change on a dime. Be it a doctor's call, a passing grade, a betrayal, a proposal, an accident, or a promotion, to expect life to remain unchanged will do nothing but create anxiety. God thought it important enough to include in His Word this idea of seasons. And when you're struggling with change, go right to God with your fear. Let Him bring peace.

He Will Transform Your Thinking

Stop imitating the ideals and opinions of the culture around you, but be inwardly transformed by the Holy Spirit through a total reformation of how you think. This will empower you to discern God's will as you live a beautiful life, satisfying and perfect in his eyes.
ROMANS 12:2 TPT

Ask the Lord to transform your mind so you don't long for the ways of this world. Ask Him to reform how you think so you're not constantly chasing the ideas and opinions of others. It's stressful to long for something that constantly eludes you. And it's uncomfortable to try to fit into a society that continues to cancel God at every turn, especially when your faith is important to you. Instead of living for the kind of acceptance the world offers, let the Lord give you discernment and wisdom to live His way. Not only will it alleviate unnecessary anxiety, but it will also empower you to live a beautiful and satisfying life that glorifies Him.

#176

Fearing the Aging Process

So no wonder we don't give up. For even though our outer person gradually wears out, our inner being is renewed every single day.
2 Corinthians 4:16 TPT

Are you anxious about the aging process? It's hard to watch our bodies change and succumb to gravity. It's sad to see our youthfulness melt away. So it is a relief to know that our inner being is renewed every single day! Because we live in a fallen world, things will fall. Things will fail. But the Lord promises that we can still find renewed joy and peace as we wake each morning. We can still have hope. Even when our bodies are feeling the effects of growing older, inside we can feel refreshed and rejuvenated because God promises it. Meditating on that promise will melt the fear away and stop the stress from robbing you of peace.

A Heavenly Perspective

We view our slight, short-lived troubles in the light of eternity. We see our difficulties as the substance that produces for us an eternal, weighty glory far beyond all comparison, because we don't focus our attention on what is seen but on what is unseen. For what is seen is temporary, but the unseen realm is eternal.
2 CORINTHIANS 4:17–18 TPT

When you decide to let the Lord's perspective be yours, you will find that peace rules in your life. Rather than stress out when trouble hits, you'll understand it will be short-lived in light of eternity. You'll be able to recognize the benefits that may come from the problems you're having to face. You will hold tight to the Lord, trusting that if He allowed this into your life, it's for a glorious purpose. It may be a daily struggle, but this life is but a breath, and you won't take this stressor with you to heaven. Friend, every fear and worry are temporary annoyances. They have no heavenly shelf-life. So ask God for His perspective, and make it your own.

#178

Learn and Listen

Wise men and women are always learning,
always listening for fresh insights.
PROVERBS 18:15 MSG

When anxiety keeps you awake at night, do you ever ask God to reveal the cause? Do you question the reason certain situations stress you out more than others? Have you ever thought about the root cause of the circumstances that make you afraid? Become a student of yourself. Let the Lord offer you fresh insights into who you are and why you respond the way you do. Chances are you'll find healing in His revelation. Maybe there are triggers He wants to remove or grace He wants to extend. Maybe there are old wounds that stir up anxiety, and the Lord desires to free you from them. God's Word says the wise always learn and listen, so be wise!

#179

The Power of His Word

Every part of Scripture is God-breathed and useful one way or another—showing us truth, exposing our rebellion, correcting our mistakes, training us to live God's way. Through the Word we are put together and shaped up for the tasks God has for us.
2 Timothy 3:16–17 msg

If God created His Word to show us truth, correct our mistakes, and train us to live His way, then chances are He will use it to help you navigate the issues causing anxiety. Have you ever spent time digging through its pages, looking for help with the struggles you're facing? Maybe God is waiting for you to sit in the Word so He can bring revelation. Maybe He is hoping you'll give Him the opportunity to bring healing. There is an immeasurable depth of goodness available to those who mine for it. You will find scriptures to address every fear and worry you're facing. So make time every day to sit with the Bible, and let it bring peace to your anxious heart.

#180

Instant Healing

*Jesus said, "Get up, take your bedroll,
start walking." The man was healed on the
spot. He picked up his bedroll and walked off.*
JOHN 5:8–9 MSG

Believe God can heal you of the spine-weakening
and spirit-breaking anxiety you're struggling with.
Trust that the Lord is able to—in an instant—
cure you of stress so it doesn't rule and ruin your
life. Just like the handicapped man Jesus healed
on the spot, you can experience the same thing if
God chooses. But friend, decide today to trust God
even if it doesn't end up being your story. Ask for
the faith to surrender to His will if the Lord decides
to not remove the anxiety. Know it's only because
it will benefit you, your testimony will bless others,
and God will be glorified. Even more, remember
His promise to help you navigate every fear and
worry so it doesn't overtake your life.

Scripture Index

OLD TESTAMENT

Exodus
14:14 . . . . #4

Deuteronomy
20:1 . . . . #167
31:6 . . . . #39
31:8 . . . . #102

Joshua
1:9 . . . . #20, #83

1 Chronicles
28:20 . . . . #166

2 Chronicles
7:14 . . . . #148

Psalms
3:6 . . . . #153
4:8 . . . . #135
16:8 . . . . #114
23:1, 4 . . . . #53

23:2–3 . . . . #52
23:4 . . . . #94
23:5–6 . . . . #54
27:1 . . . . #48
27:2–3 . . . . #169
27:11 . . . . #170
27:13–14 . . . . #171
32:8–9 . . . . #26
32:10 . . . . #27
34:1–3 . . . . #65
34:4 . . . . #34
34:7 . . . . #168
34:12–14 . . . . #64
34:15, 17–18 . . . . . . #63
37:1 . . . . #118
37:7 . . . . #37
37:8–9 . . . . #38
37:19 . . . . #112
38:4 . . . . #127
38:9 . . . . #128
38:9–10 . . . . #125

38:10–11 . . . . #130
38:15 . . . . #133
38:21–22 . . . . #129
46:1–2 . . . . #8
46:10 . . . . #71
55:22–23 . . . . #22
56:1–2 . . . . #145
56:1–4 . . . . #32
56:3 . . . . #92
56:3–4 . . . . #146
62:5–6 . . . . #7
62:8 . . . . #3
63:2 . . . . #147
91:1–2 . . . . #59
91:3 . . . . #120
91:4 . . . . #121
91:5–6 . . . . #60
91:7–8 . . . . #122
91:9–10 . . . . #123
91:11–13 . . . . #61
91:14 . . . . #126
91:15–16 . . . . #62
94:4–5 . . . . #172
94:16–19 . . . . #30
94:18–19 . . . . #86
103:5 . . . . #154
103:8–9 . . . . #155

103:12 . . . . #156
103:14 . . . . #157
103:22 . . . . #158
112:7 . . . . #164
112:8 . . . . #165
118:6–7 . . . . #149
119:165 . . . . #139
121:1–2 . . . . #51
138:7–8 . . . . #100
139:7–10 . . . . #69
139:17–18 . . . . #70
139:23–24 . . . . #68
145:8 . . . . #13

Proverbs
3:5–6 . . . . #23
12:15 . . . . #144
12:25 . . . . #29
17:22 . . . . #73
18:15 . . . . #178
19:20 . . . . #143
29:25 . . . . #55

Ecclesiastes
3:1 . . . . #174

Isaiah
26:3 . . . . #40, #87

35:3–4	. . . .	#105
35:4	. . . .	#47
40:31	. . . .	#72
41:10	. . . .	#28
41:11–12	. . . .	#89
41:13	. . . .	#88
43:1	. . . .	#49
43:2	. . . .	#33
54:17	. . . .	#150

Jeremiah

17:7–8	. . . .	#85
17:9–10	. . . .	#36
29:11	. . . .	#24

Lamentations

3:22–23	. . . .	#10
3:55–57	. . . .	#161

Joel

2:13	. . . .	#151

Zephaniah

3:17	. . . .	#163

NEW TESTAMENT

Matthew

6:1	. . . .	#117
6:19	. . . .	#119
6:24	. . . .	#137
6:25	. . . .	#76
6:25, 27	. . . .	#17
6:26	. . . .	#77
6:27	. . . .	#78
6:28–30	. . . .	#79
6:31–33	. . . . .	#46, #80
6:34	. . . .	#25
11:28–30	. . . .	#6
13:22	. . . .	#113
14:27	. . . .	#162
14:31	. . . .	#124
17:8	. . . .	#152
19:26	. . . .	#5
28:20	. . . .	#12

Mark

13:11	. . . .	#106

Luke

1:37	. . . .	#82
10:40	. . . .	#56

10:41–42 ..... #57, #91
12:22–23 .... #50
12:25 .... #84
21:34 .... #131

John
3:16–17 .... #104
5:8–9 .... #180
13:34–35 .... #1
14:1 .... #81
14:27 .... #18
16:32–33 .... #58
16:33 .... #93

Romans
5:1 .... #138
8:6 .... #110
8:26–27 .... #45
8:28 .... #99
8:31 .... #97
8:32 .... #109
12:2 .... #175
12:18–19 .... #134
15:13 .... #95

1 Corinthians
14:33 .... #140

2 Corinthians
4:16 .... #176
4:17–18 .... #177
9:8 .... #103
12:9 .... #159
12:10 .... #101

Galatians
6:9–10 .... #90

Ephesians
3:18–19 .... #11
4:29 .... #98
4:31–32 .... #132
5:15 .... #142
5:16 .... #160

Philippians
1:6 .... #42
4:6–7 .... #15
4:8–9 .... #41
4:19 .... #44

Colossians
3:2 .... #115
3:15–17 .... #35

2 Thessalonians
3:16 . . . . #67

2 Timothy
1:7 . . . . #2, #19
3:16–17 . . . . #179

Hebrews
11:1–2 . . . . #96
13:5–6 . . . . #9
13:8 . . . . #173

James
1:2–4 . . . . #74
1:5–8 . . . . #31
1:12 . . . . #75
1:13 . . . . #107
1:19–20 . . . . #108
3:18 . . . . #141

1 Peter
3:11 . . . . #136
3:14 . . . . #111
5:6–7 . . . . #16
5:10 . . . . #21

1 John
1:9 . . . . #14

4:18 . . . . #43

Revelation
21:4 . . . . #66, #116

Looking for More Encouragement for Your Heart?

Worry Less, Pray More

This purposeful devotional guide features 180 readings and prayers designed to help alleviate your worries as you learn to live in the peace of the Almighty God, who offers calm for your anxiety-filled soul.

Paperback / 978-1-68322-861-5 / $4.99

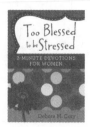

Too Blessed to be Stressed: 3-Minute Devotions for Women

You'll find the spiritual pick-me-up you need in *Too Blessed to Be Stressed: 3-Minute Devotions for Women*. 180 uplifting readings from bestselling author Debora M. Coty pack a powerful dose of inspiration, encouragement, humor, and faith into just-right-sized readings for your busy schedule.

Paperback / 978-1-63409-569-3 / $4.99